MCSA Cloud Infrastructure Lab Guide: 70-534 Exam Architecting Microsoft Azure Solutions

Harinder Kohli

This edition has been published by arrangement with **Amazon CreateSpace**.

ISBN
ISBN-13: 978-1544160627
ISBN-10: 1544160623

Edition: 2017

Table of Contents

Introduction

Having Designed Technology solutions for last 25 years I found that to be good designer you require three fundamental skills- Technical Design, Technical Implementation and Designing Customer Solutions taking into account Customer Business Process, Outcomes and Constraints.

Though 70-534 is a design exam but to be good designer you need to have hands on experience. Technical Implementation experience allows you to implement solution using different options and see how various solution components work together. This experience allows one to design solution in multiple ways. Real world design is not about the best practice design. In real world you need to design the solution with conflicting requirements and multiple constraints imposed by the customer.

When I started preparing for 70-534 exam, Architecting Azure Solution I already had cloud design experience and knowledge about how cloud can be used in various Industry Domains & Verticals. What I was lacking was hands on experience with Azure cloud.

There were no guides available for hands on practice. Most of the Azure books available were outdated as they were written with classic portal where as Microsoft was transitioning to New portal. I started with Classic Portal and then when I moved to New Portal it was all confusing.

I started lab practice and started taking notes of all labs. I used Azure Documentation, hands on with Azure Portal & some free books from Microsoft Press. This book is outcome of all those efforts.

My design knowledge with Azure was increasing as I was writing this book. I hope after reading and doing all labs your design and implementation knowledge can move to next level.

The Book covers most of the lab topics including labs for Networking, Compute, Storage, Azure Active Directory, Azure Backup, SQL Database, Security Center, Operational Management Suite (OMS), Web Apps & Load Balancing. Labs for Hybrid Cloud are also included like Managing on Premises Servers and taking Backup of on Premises Servers

The best way to use the book is to first read about a topic in Azure Documentation, White Papers, Azure Books and then do the labs from this book.

Refresh your kindle book library regularly as I will be updating the book regularly.

I would be pleased to hear your feedback and thoughts on the book. Please comment on Amazon or mail to: harinder-kohli@outlook.com.

Harinder Kohli

Chapter 1 - Signing to Azure & Lab Tricks

Azure Sign up

1. Go to **https://azure.microsoft.com/en-us/free**
2. You will require MS email id, valid credit card and Mobile Number for verification.
3. You will get USD 200 Azure credit with 30 days validity. Remember any balance left in your Azure credit will expire after 30 days. Make full use of your free credits.

Lab Tricks

1. During your practice you will be creating many resources. The best way to locate a resource and go to resource dashboard is to Click All Resources in left pane.
2. After completing a lab don t proceed to next lab. Instead check for other options and information available.
3. After you enable Security Center don t proceed with the lab immediately because it takes at least 2-3 hours for all Recommendations to become available.
4. Use only lowercase letters for names of the resources. I used a combination of uppercase and lowercase letters and it became confusing.
5. Use a single password for all VM accounts and user accounts. Not valid if it s a live production site.
6. If you stop and start your Windows VM make sure to download the RDP file again as the IP address is changed.

Chapter 2 – Topologies & Resources

Topology 1

Topology 1 will be the main topology. We will build this topology as we progress through the Chapter labs. This topology is applicable for the all chapters.

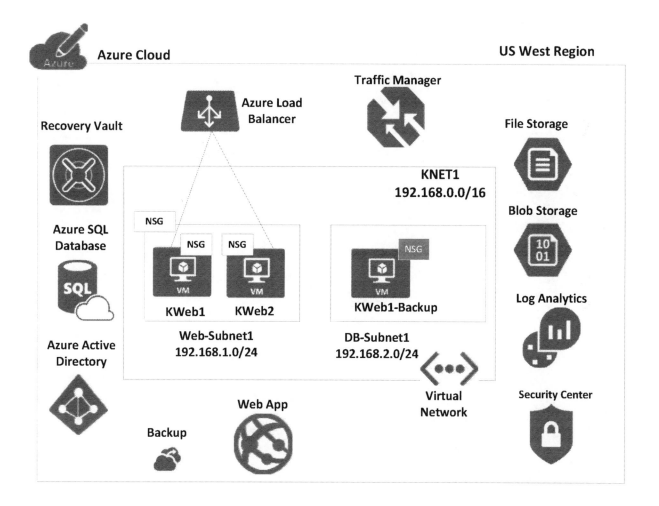

Topology 2

Topology 2 will be used in Chapter 8 - Azure SQL Database.

US West

US East

Replication

Primary Database kworks1
Kdb1 Server

Secondary Database kworks1
Kdb2 Server

Topology 3

Topology 3 will be used in Chapter 13   Global Load Balancing with Traffic Manager.

Traffic Manger

Europe West

US West

Europe West Web App

US West Web App

Resources

Most of the lab configuration will be done by using following resources. Readers will be creating them as they progress through labs. Readers need not use the similar names.

1. Region: US West
2. Resource Group: KR1
3. Virtual Network: KNET1
4. Subnet: Web-Subnet1 and DB-Subnet1
5. Availability Group: KAS1
6. Virtual Machine: KWeb1
7. Storage Account: kstorgps1
8. OMS work space: Koms
9. Web App: Kwebapp1

All labs resources are created in US West region. In chapter 8 Secondary Database was created in US East and in chapter 13 Europe West Web App was created in Europe West.

Chapter 3 – Networking

Azure Virtual Network (VNET)

An Azure virtual network (VNET) is Virtual Data Center in the cloud. You can further segment virtual network (VNET) into subnets. Access to the subnets can be controlled using Network Security groups. You can define the IP address blocks, security policies, and route tables within this network. Virtual Machines are created in Virtual Networks.

In this chapter we will create below topology. Default Azure AD is created when you sign for Azure subscription.

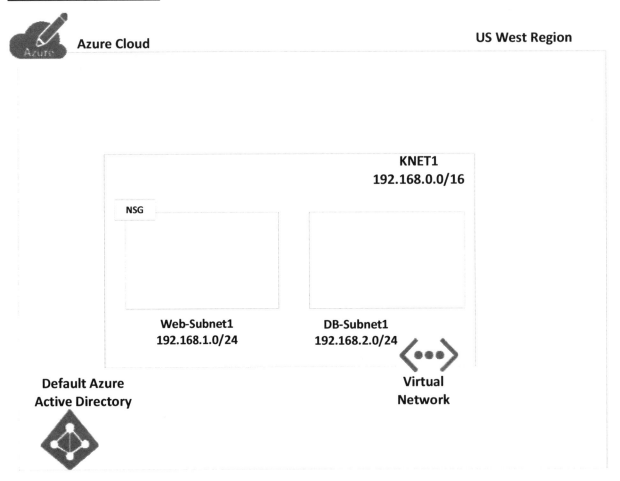

We will create following in the Networking labs:

1. Virtual Network : KNET1
2. Subnet: Web-Subnet1 & DB-Subnet1
3. Network Security Group: KNSG1 & Assign it to Web-Subnet1
4. Adding http & RDP allow rule in Network Security Group KNSG1
5. Availability set KAS1.

Note: DB-Subnet1 is just for demonstration only. No Database VM will be installed here. We will be using Azure SQL Database which is cloud DBaaS.

Lab 1: Creating Azure virtual network (VNET)

1. **https://portal.azure.com.**
2. Click + New > Networking > Virtual network.

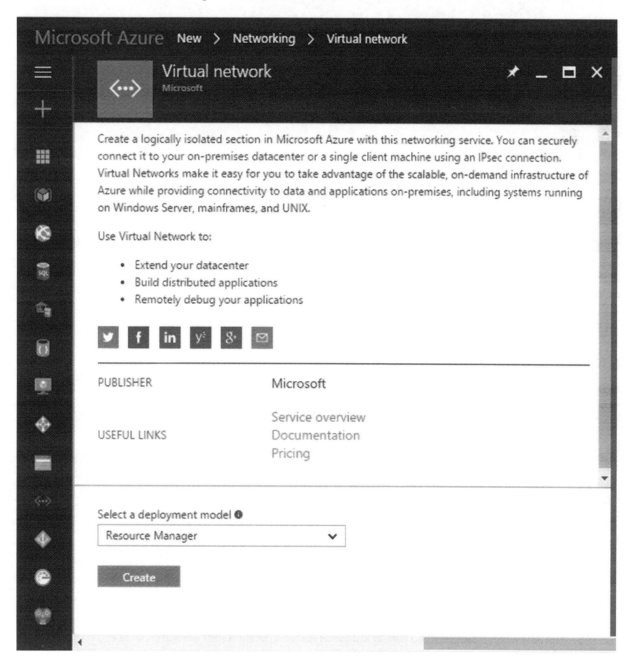

3. Select Resource Manager and click create.

4. In the Create virtual network blade enter the following:

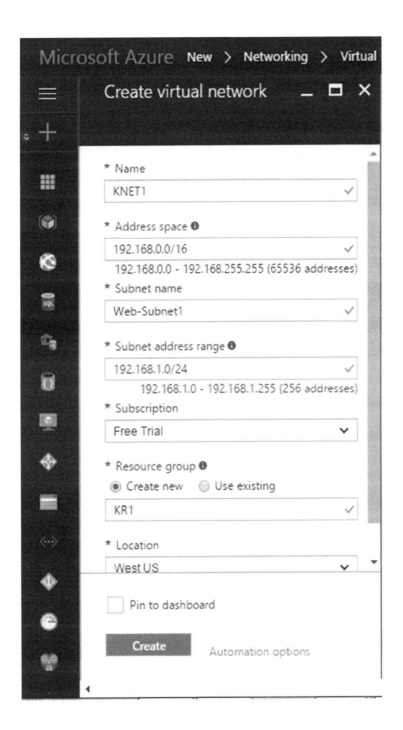

5. Click Create. It will take up to 45 seconds for VNET deployment to complete.

Lab 2: Creating Second Subnet

1. Click All Resources 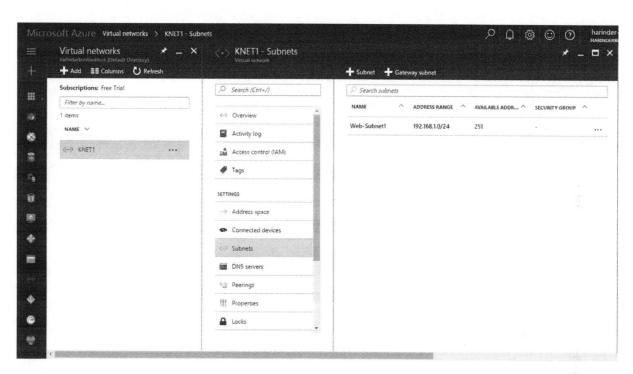. Click KNET1. Under settings click Subnets.

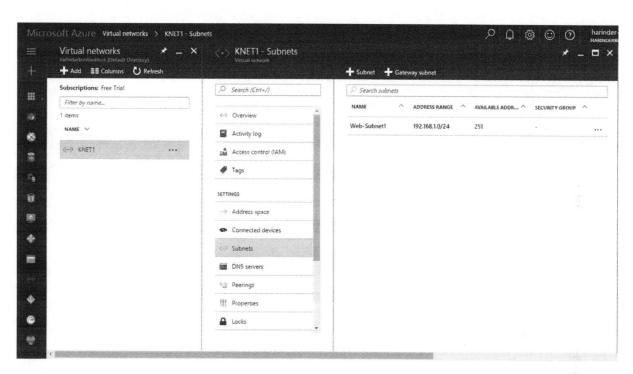

2. Click +Subnet. In Add Subnet blade enter following and click ok.

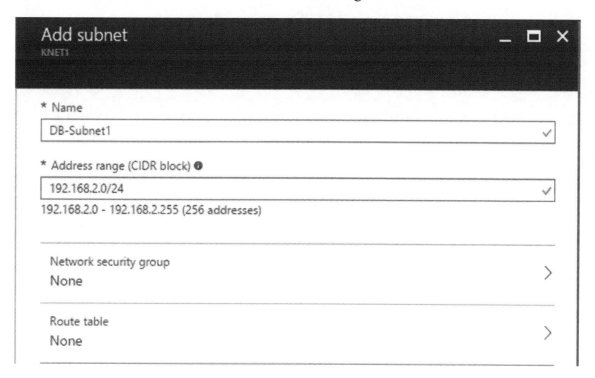

Network Security Groups (NSG)

Network Security Groups control access to the subnet. NSG act as Firewall between Subnets. They can also be used to control Internet-bound traffic on the virtual subnet. Note: NSG can be applied both at Subnet level and at VM NIC Level.

Lab 3: Creating Network Security Group KNSG1

1. **https://portal.azure.com**
2. Click + New > Networking>Network Security Group. Select Resource Manager.

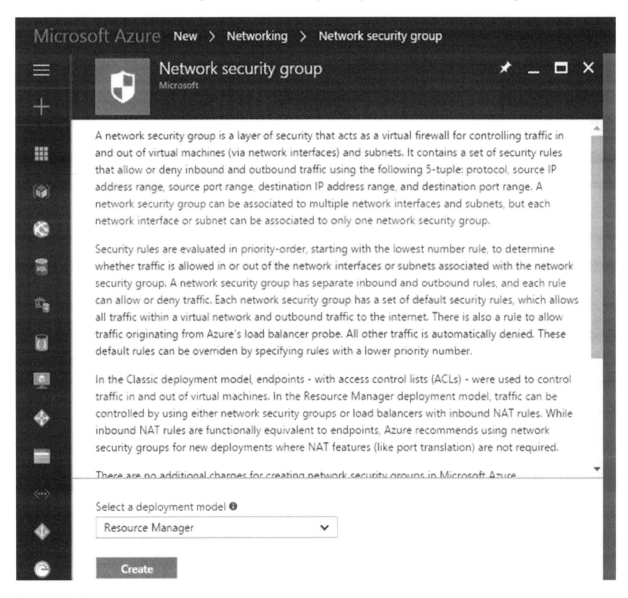

3. Click Create.

4. In the Create network security group blade enter the following:

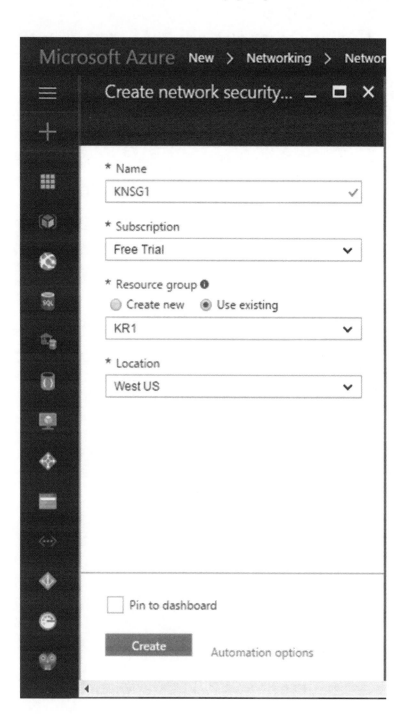

5. Click Create. It will take up to 45 seconds for deployment to complete.

Lab 4: Assigning Network security group KNSG1 to the Web-Subnet1

1. Click All Resources ▦ . Click KNET1. Under settings click Subnets.

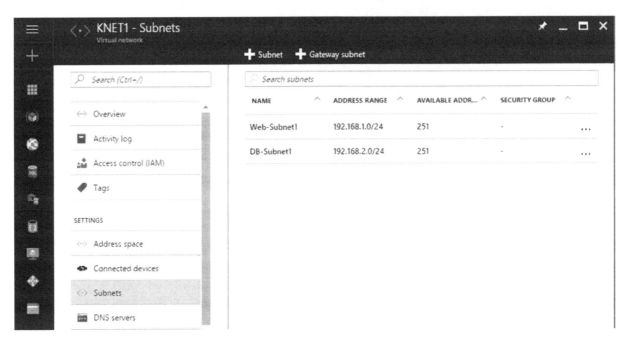

2. Click Web-Subnet1.

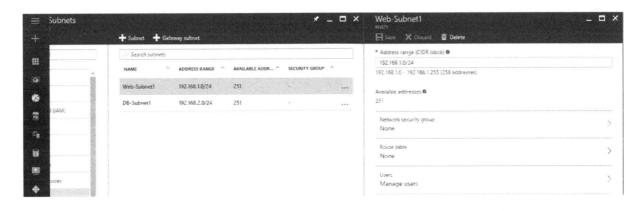

3. In the Web-Subnet1 blade click Network Security Group. Select KNSG1.

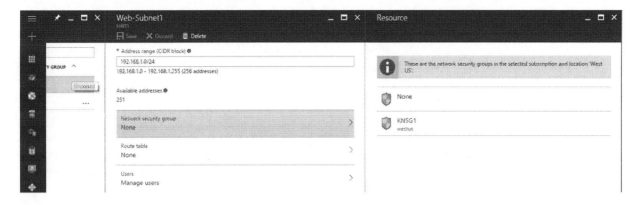

4. Click Save.

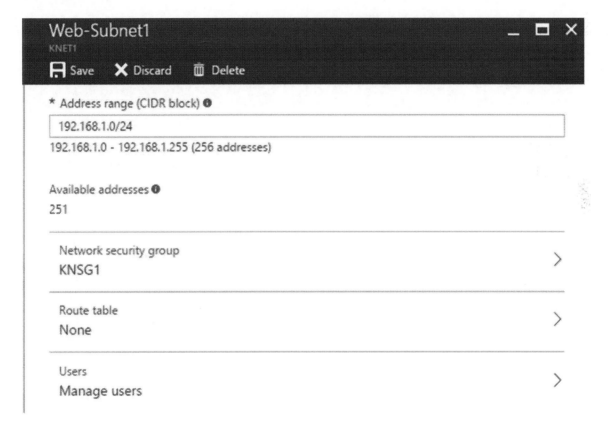

Lab 5: Adding http & RDP allow rule in Network Security Group KNSG1

1. Click All Resources >Click NSG KNSG1>Click Inbound security rules>Check Default Rules>the default NSG rule stops all inbound internet traffic to the subnets>Adding inbound http and RDP allow rule will enable Windows Web VM in Web-Subnet1 to be accessed from Internet through http and RDP.

2. **Adding http rule**>Click + Add>In Add inbound security rule blade enter following.

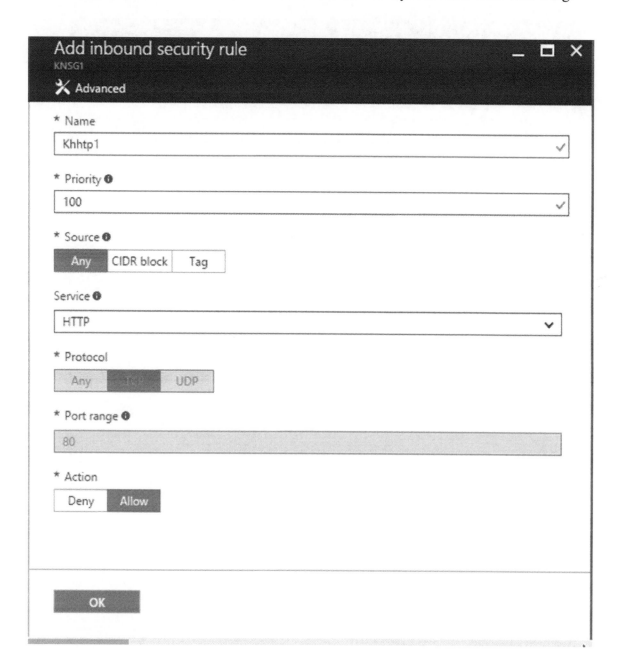

3. **Adding RDP Rule**>Click + Add. In Add inbound security rule blade enter following.

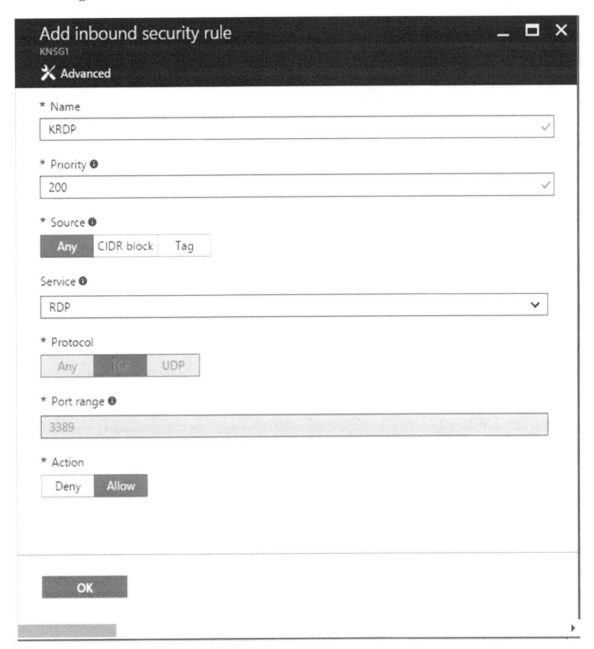

Design Nugget

1. By default NSG at VM level allows inbound RDP. But NSG at Subnet level does not allow inbound RDP.
2. NSG create two level of security. One at subnet level and other at VM level.
3. We can have different options for subnet NSG and VM NSG to protects our Virtual Machines.

Availability Set (AS)

By creating an Availability Set and adding virtual machines to the AS, Azure will ensure that the Virtual Machines in the set get distributed across the physical hosts, Network switch & Rack in such a way that a hardware failure will not bring down all the machines in the set.

Lab 6: Creating Availability Set

1. https://portal.azure.com
2. Click + New > In the search box type Availability Set and Press enter.
3. Click Availability Set. Click Create.
4. On the Create availability set blade enter following information and click create.

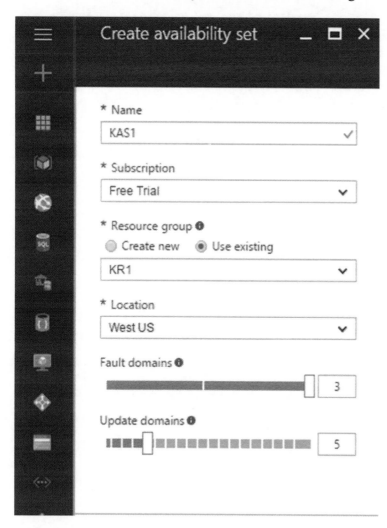

Design Nugget

1. Fault Domain will place VMs in Different racks and Update domain will place VMs in different host.

Chapter 4 - Compute

Azure Compute instance is a web service that provides resizable compute capacity in the cloud.
Azure Compute instance comes in different families: A series, D Series, F Series etc.
Two drives are created in Virtual Server by default. One is C Drive and other is D Drive. D
Drive is temporary drive and is located on host where the Virtual Server is running. C drive is
Operating System drive and is accessed over the network.

<u>In this chapter we will add Virtual Machine KWeb1 to the topology.</u>

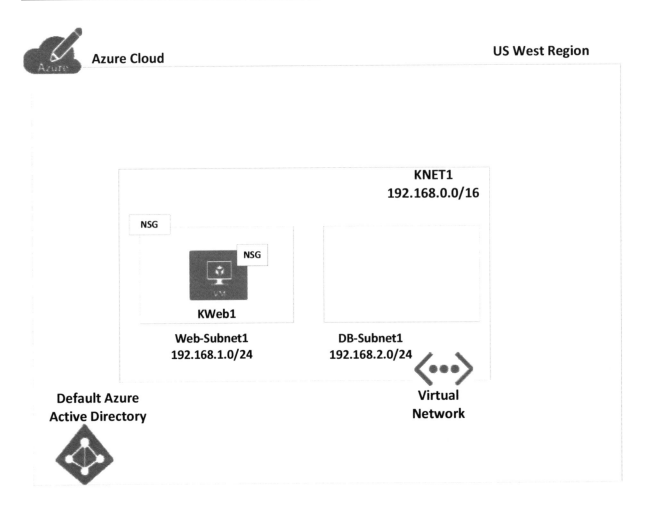

<u>We will create following in the Compute labs:</u>

1. Create KWeb1 VM in Web-Subnet1.We will also configure KWeb1 VM Network Security
   Group for inbound Internet access.
2. Install IIS on KWeb1 and access the default website.
3. Add Data disk to KWeb1 VM.

4. We will be using Windows Server 2016 with SQL Server 2016 Express image. This will also install SQL Server Management Studio (SSMS) on the VM. SSMS will be used to connect to Azure Database in later labs

Lab 7: Creating Azure Windows Compute Instance

1. Click + New > In the search box type SQL Server 2016 Express and press enter.
2. In the result choose SQL Server 2016 SP1 Express on Windows Server 2016.
3. Select Resource Manager and click create>Specify Following.

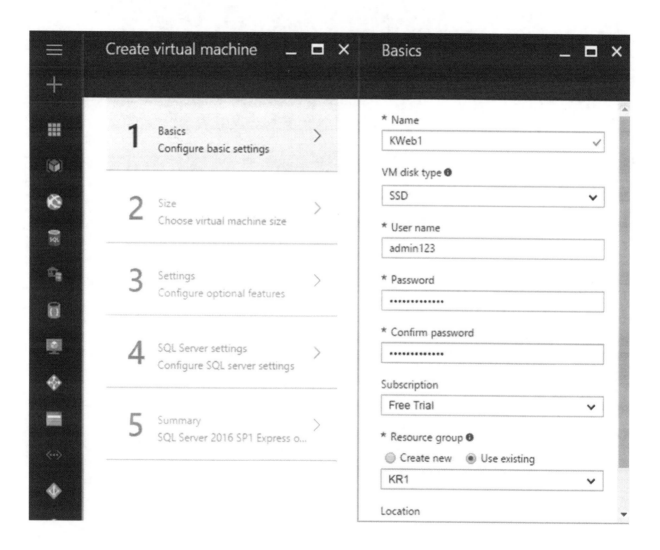

4. In create virtual machine blade size settings click View All and Select DS1_V2.

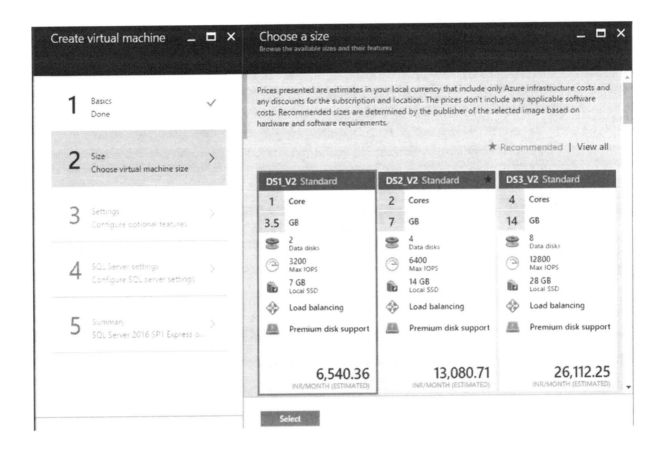

5. In create virtual machine blade settings select default values for storage account, Public IP Address and Network Security group. For Virtual Network select KNET1, for Subnet select Web-Subnet1 and For Availability Set select KAS1. (You need to scroll down for AS).

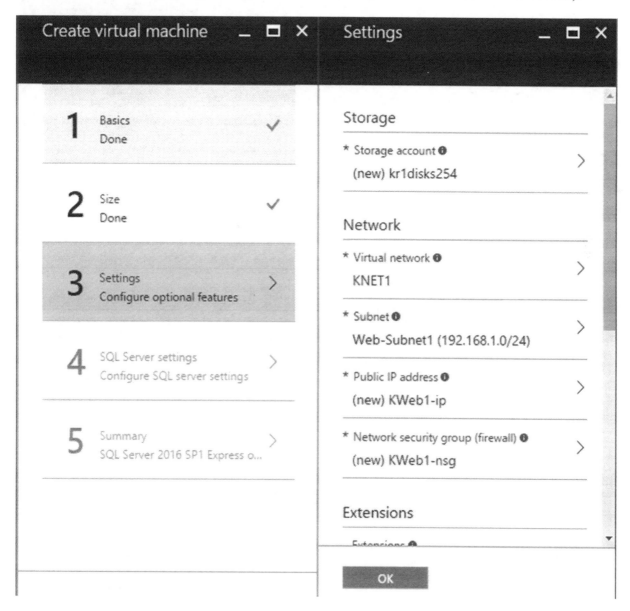

Note 1: NSG KWeb1-nsg is applied at VM NIC level.
Note 2: By default NSG KWeb1-nsg allows inbound RDP from internet. In later lab we will allow inbound http to the web VM.
Note 3: Now you have 2 NSG. One at Subnet level and one at VM NIC level.
Note 4: Subnet level NSG is optional.

6. In create virtual machine blade SQL Server Settings enter following:

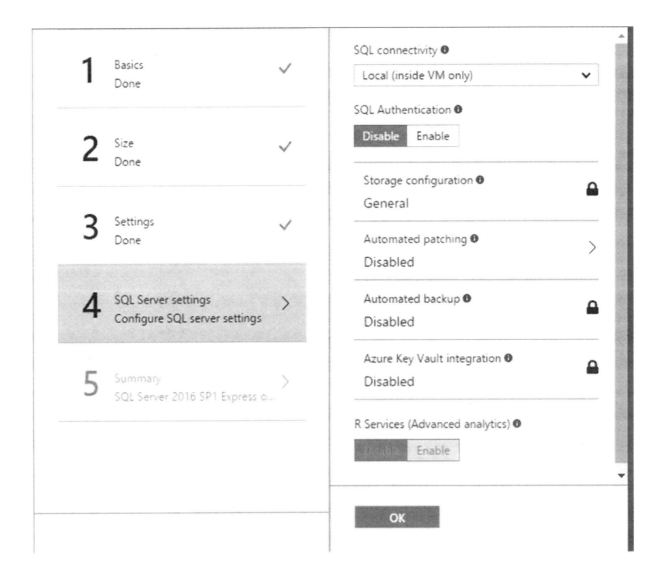

7. In create virtual machine blade Summary click ok. It will take around 15 Minutes to deploy.

Lab 8: Connecting to the Azure Instance

1. Go to KWeb1 VM Dashboard> click connect and it will download RDP file with IP address of KWeb1 VM.

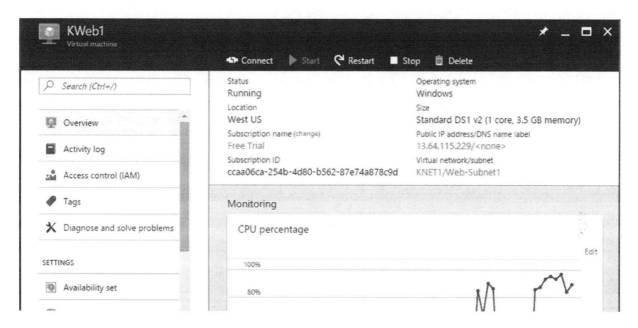

2. Click the downloaded RDP file. Enter username and password.

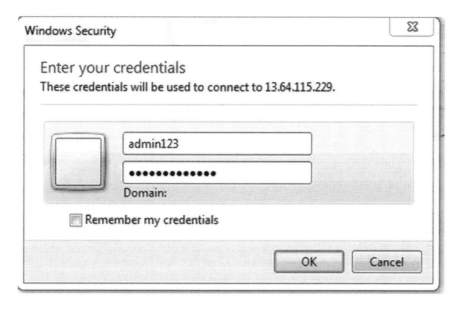

3. This will open RDP connection to KWeb1 VM from your desktop.

Lab 9: Installing IIS web server in KWeb1 VM

1. Connect to KWeb1 VM using RDP.
2. Open server Manager> Click add roles and features
3. In the Add Roles and Features Wizard, on the Installation Type page, choose Role-based or feature-based installation, and then click Next.
4. Select KWeb1 VM from the server pool and click Next.
5. On the Server Roles page, select Web Server (IIS).
6. In the pop-up about adding features needed for IIS, make sure that Include management tools is selected and then click Add Features. When the pop-up closes, click Next in the wizard.
7. next, next, next, next.
8. Install.
9. It will take around 1 minute to install the IIS. After Installation is complete click close.

Lab 10: Adding http inbound rule in the KWeb1 VM NSG

1. Click All Resources> Select and click Network Security group KWeb1-nsg which is associated with KWeb1 VM.

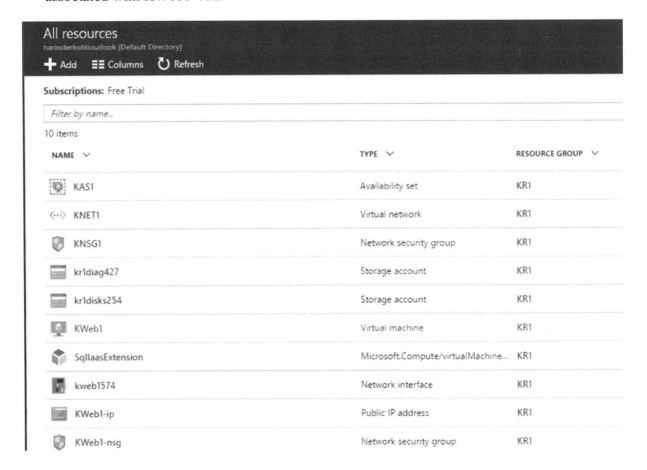

2. Click Inbound security Rules. Note the default rdp allow rule.

3. Click +Add and Enter following information and click ok.

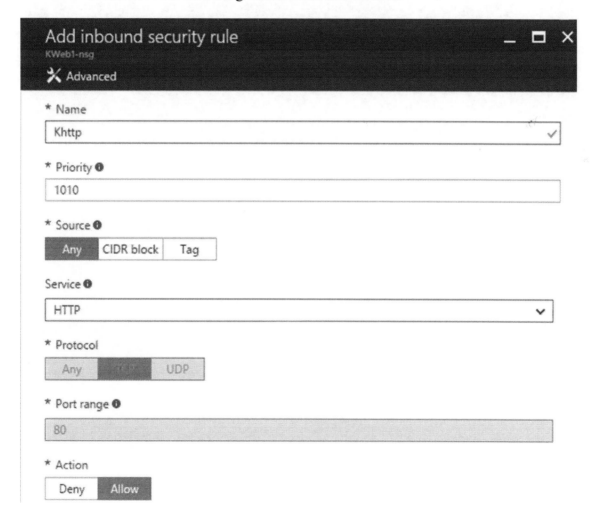

Lab 11: Connecting to Default IIS website on KWeb1 VM

1. Go to KWeb1 VM dashboard. Note down KWeb1 VM IP address
2. Open a browser and type: http://13.64.115.229

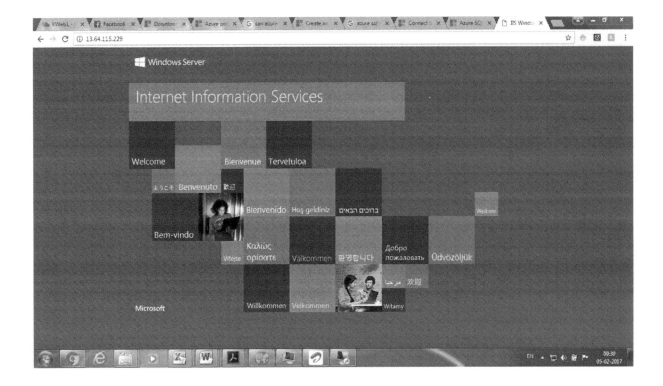

Lab 12: Adding Data Disk to KWeb1 VM

1. Go to KWeb1 VM pane. Click Disks

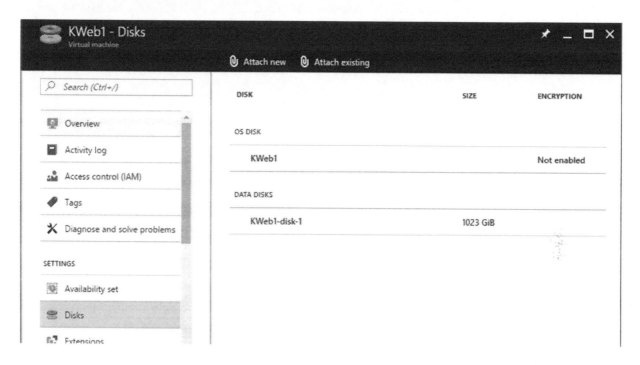

2. Click Attach new and enter following and click ok.

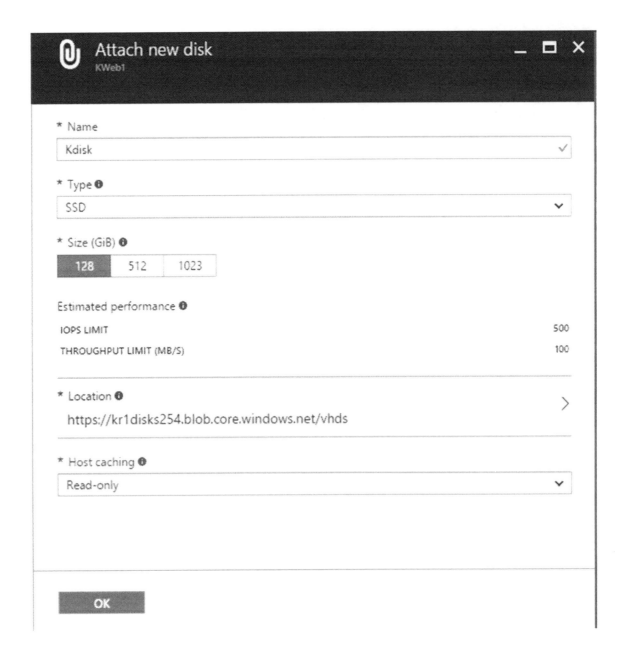

Lab 13: Initialize the Data Disk in Windows Server

1. Connect to KWeb1 VM using RDP.
2. Open Server Manager. In the left pane, select File and Storage Services.
3. The Disks section lists the disks. In most cases, it will have disk 0, disk 1, disk 2, disk 3, disk 4 etc. The Disk 0 is the operating system Disk. Disk 1 is the temporary disk. The Data disk you just added will list the Partition as Unknown. Right-click the data disk and select Initialize. Once complete, the Partition will be listed as GPT.

Chapter 5 - Azure Storage

Azure Storage

Azure Storage is the cloud storage solution. Azure Storage is highly available and massively scalable to meet the demands of modern applications like Big Data, Media Solution etc.

Azure Provides four types of storage - Blob, Table, Queue and Files.

Azure Storage Accounts

An Azure storage account provides a unique namespace to store and access your Azure Storage data objects.There are two types of storage accounts: General-purpose Storage Accounts & Blob Storage Accounts.

General-Purpose Storage Accounts

General-purpose storage account has two performance tiers:

1. A standard storage performance tier which allows you to store Tables, Queues, Files, Blobs and Azure virtual machine disks. **It is backed by magnetic disks.**
2. A premium storage performance tier which currently only supports Azure virtual machine disks. **It is backed by SSD.**

Blob Storage account

Blob Storage account are specialised for storing blob data and support choosing an access tier. Blob storage accounts support only block and append blobs, and not page blobs.
Access Tier - Hot & Cool

Replication Options

The data in your Microsoft Azure storage account is always replicated to ensure high availability. There are four types of replication options.
Locally redundant storage (LRS)
Zone-redundant storage (ZRS)
Geo-redundant storage (GRS)
Read-access geo-redundant storage (RA-GRS)

In this chapter we will add Blob and File Storage to the topology.

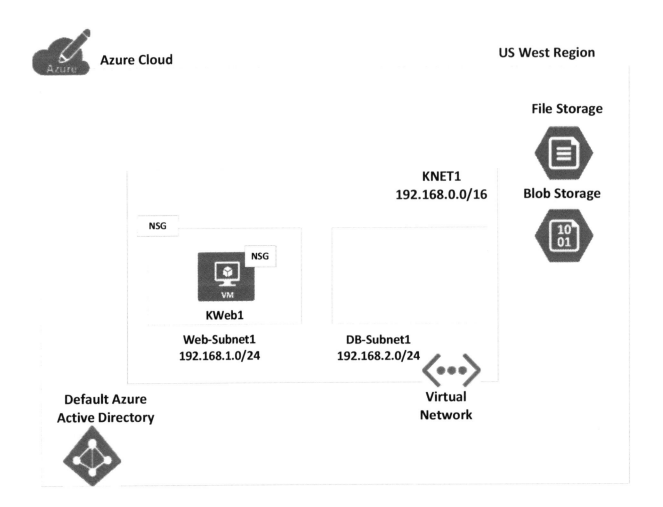

We will create following in the Storage labs:

1. Create Storage account kstorgps1
2. In Blob storage we will create container and add file to it and access the file over the internet.
3. We will change the access policy in container to private and check whether file can be accessed over the internet or not
4. Create File Share and mount it to KWeb1 Windows VM

Lab 14: Creating storage Account

1. https://portal.azure.com
2. Click + New >Storage> Storage Account

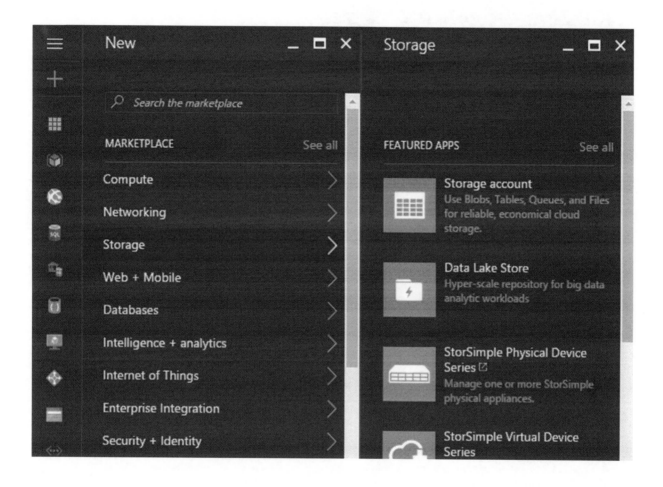

3. In the create Storage account blade enter following and click create.

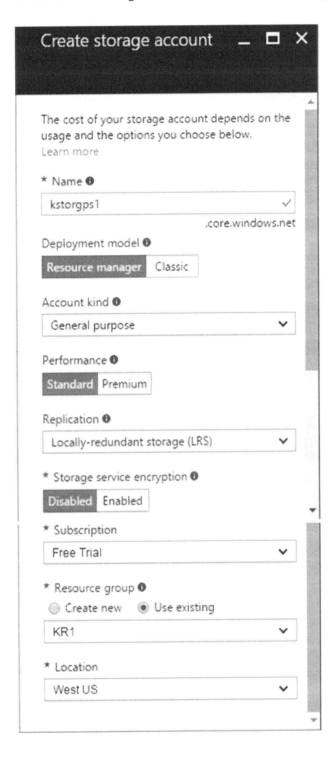

Lab 15: Create container using Blobs and upload a file

1. Create Hello World text file with Hello world as content on your desktop. We will upload this file to Azure Blob storage.

2. Click All Resources in left Pane>Select Storage Account kstorgps1 and click Blobs.

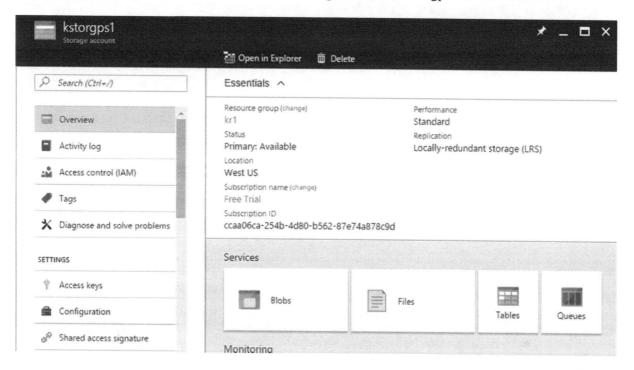

3. Click +container

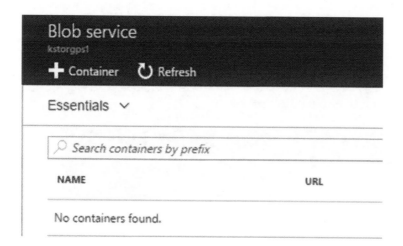

4. In New Container Blade specify following and click create. Choosing Access type as blob. This will allows files to be accessed from internet.

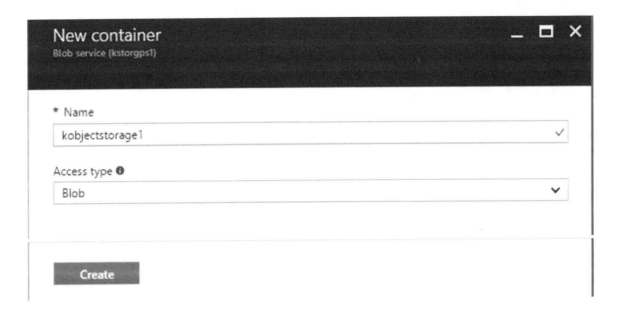

5. Click on newly created container kobjectstorage1

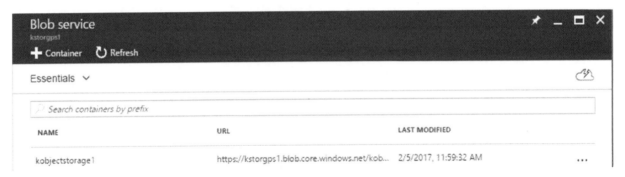

6. Click on container kobjectstorage1 and then click on upload.

7. In upload blob blade enter following. Upload Hello world.txt file and click upload.

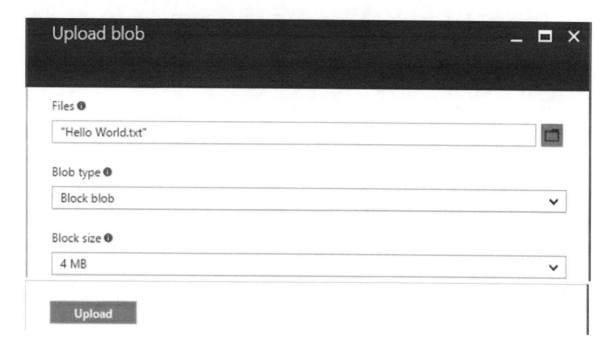

8. In kobjectstorage1 container double click Hello world.txt

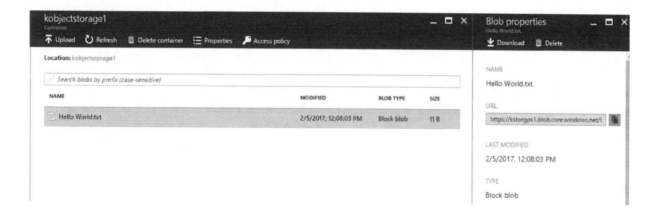

9. In Blob properties copy the URL of Hello world.txt.

10. https://kstorgps1.blob.core.windows.net/kobjectstorage1/Hello%20World.txt

11. **You can access Hello world.txt over internet when access policy is Blob.**

12. Change the access policy to private. Click Access Policy

13. Choose Access Policy as private from drop down box and click Save.

14. In Blob properties copy the URL of Hello world.txt.

15. https://kstorgps1.blob.core.windows.net/kobjectstorage1/Hello%20World.txt

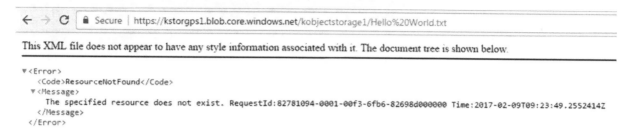

This XML file does not appear to have any style information associated with it. The document tree is shown below.

```
▼<Error>
   <Code>ResourceNotFound</Code>
   ▼<Message>
      The specified resource does not exist. RequestId:82781094-0001-00f3-6fb6-82698d000000 Time:2017-02-09T09:23:49.2552414Z
   </Message>
</Error>
```

16. Now you cannot access Hello world.txt after access policy is changed to private.

Lab 16: Create File Share and mount to Windows VM KWeb1

1. Click All Resources >Select Storage Account kstorgps1. In kstorgps1 pane click Access keys and copy Primary access key.
2. In kstorgps1 pane click Files.

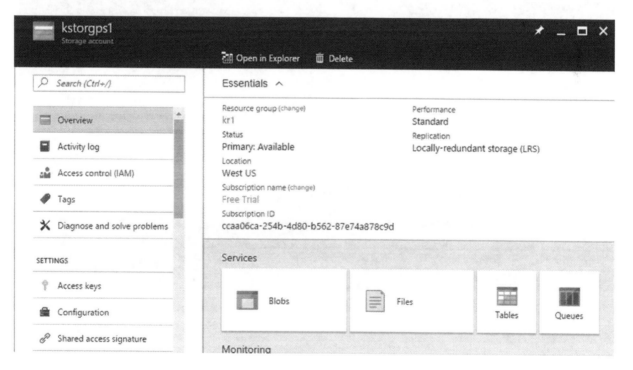

3. Click +File share and enter following and click create.

4. kfileshare1 is created. Double click kfileshare1

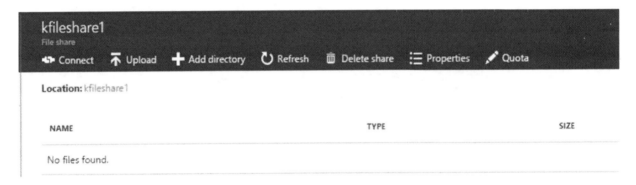

5. Click upload. In upload files blade upload Hello World.txt from desktop and click upload.

6. Click Connect in kfileshare1.

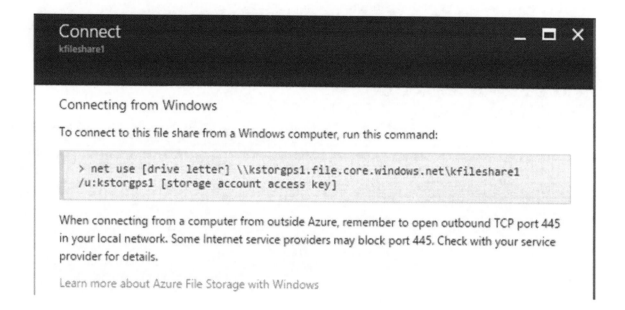

Connect
kfileshare1

Connecting from Windows

To connect to this file share from a Windows computer, run this command:

```
> net use [drive letter] \\kstorgps1.file.core.windows.net\kfileshare1
/u:kstorgps1 [storage account access key]
```

When connecting from a computer from outside Azure, remember to open outbound TCP port 445 in your local network. Some Internet service providers may block port 445. Check with your service provider for details.

Learn more about Azure File Storage with Windows

7. Connect to KWeb1 using RDP. Run the above command in cmd of KWeb1.
   Replace drive letter with z: and Storage account access key with
   XV25uxADU3hbq9UQXpkTBDIkI1l8fk4bLUDp76kTBybWQXIruuFJpN2i3Ri13MnyqOfP
   bpnrILLzIW1ZDtu8uQ==

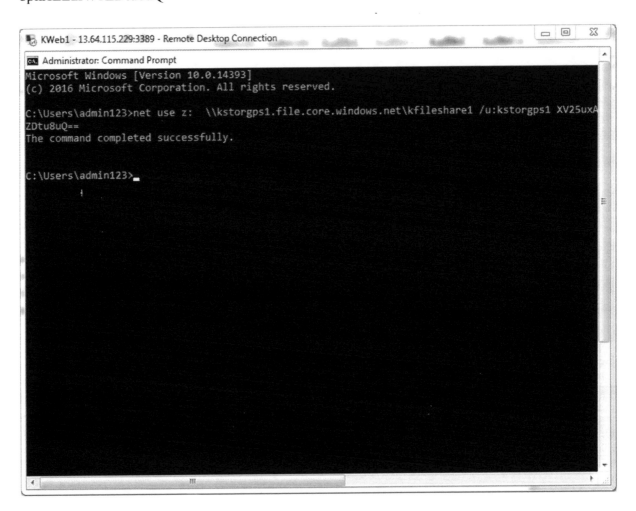

8. Go to File Explorer in KWeb1 VM>You can see the kfileshare1 mounted.

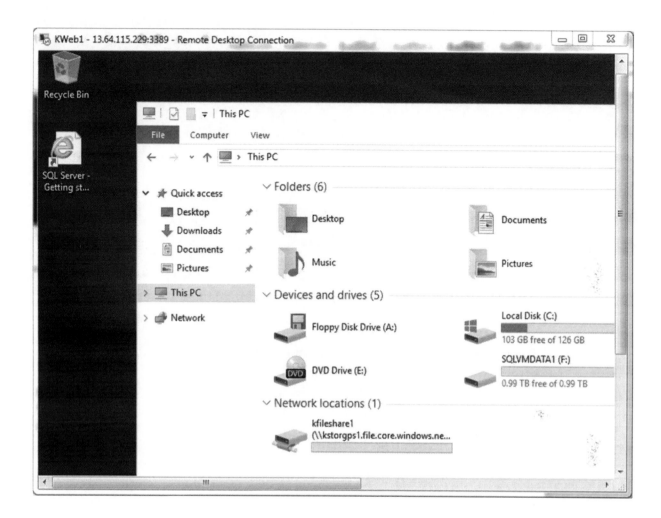

Chapter 6 - Azure Active Directory

Microsoft Azure Active Directory (Azure AD) is a cloud-based identity & access management solution.
A default Azure AD is created with the subscription.
Azure AD comes in 3 Tiers: Free, Basic and Premium.

You can synchronise Azure Active Directory with on Prem Active Directory Domain Services using AD Connect.

Azure AD supports other identity providers like Facebook, Hotmail, Google, Linkedin etc.
Azure AD supports on prem AD Domain services as identity provider using ADFS.

Azure AD supports single sign-on to SaaS Applications.

Azure Active Directory Premium supports additional features such as MFA, Self Service Password Reset with on premises write back, AD Connect health, Identity Protection & Identity Management.

Azure Active Directory B2C is an identity and access management cloud solution for consumer-facing web and mobile applications.
With Azure Active Directory B2C, Consumers can sign up for applications by using their existing social accounts Facebook, Google, Amazon, LinkedIn.

Azure Active Directory (Azure AD) B2B collaboration lets you enable access to your corporate applications by partner employees using partner-managed identities.
Your business partners use their own sign-in credentials, which frees you from managing an external partner directory.

Note: Most of the Azure AD configuration will happen in Classic Portal

In this chapter we will Configure the default Azure Active Directory which was created when we signed for the Azure Subscription.

We will create following in the Azure Active Directory labs

1. Create user and add them to Azure Resource KWeb1 VM
2. Create 2 users
3. Create Group and add the users created in Step 2
4. Add the group to Storage Account Kstorgps1
5. Single Sign-on for SaaS Applications (Twitter)

Lab 17: Creating User in AAD for managing KWeb1 VM

1. **https://manage.windowsazure.com/** (Classic Portal)
2. Go to Default directory and click Manage Access.

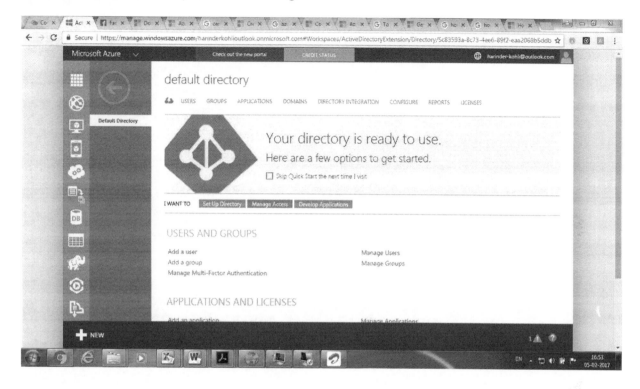

3. Click Add a user. Add User Blade opens and enter following information:

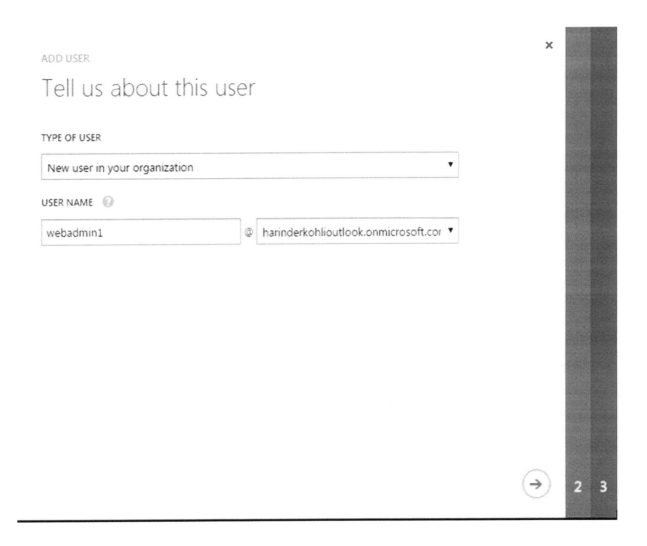

4. Click arrow and User Profile blade opens.

5. Enter Following in User Profile Blade

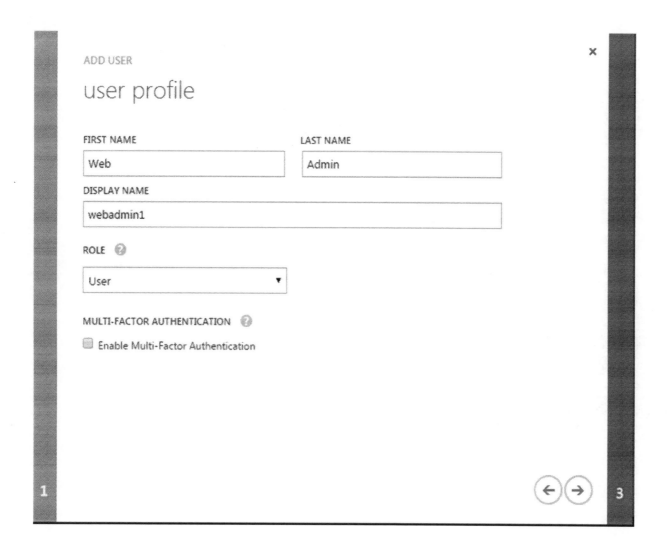

6. Click arrow and Temporary password blade opens.

7. In Temporary Password Blade click create and note down the password.

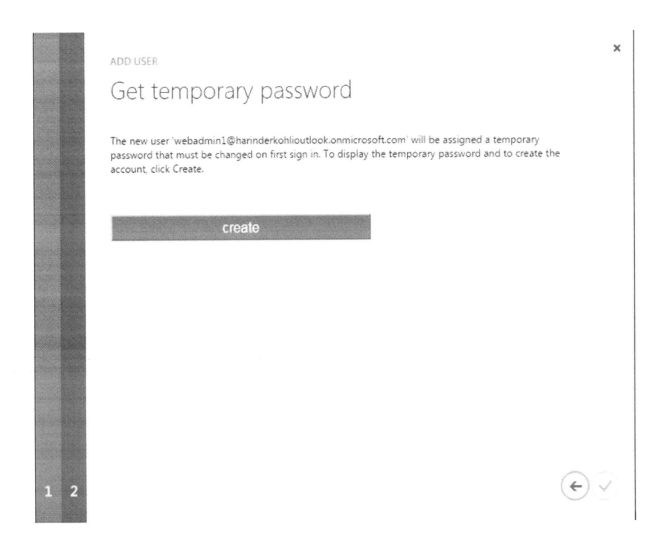

8. user login name will be webadmin1@harinderkohlioutlook.onmicrosoft.com
9. Log on to azure portal as webadmin1@harinderkohlioutlook.onmicrosoft.com with temporary credential and then change the temporary password.

Lab 18: Adding webadmin1 User to KWeb1 VM Resource

1. Go to KWeb1 VM pane and click Access control (IAM). Note the default admin user.

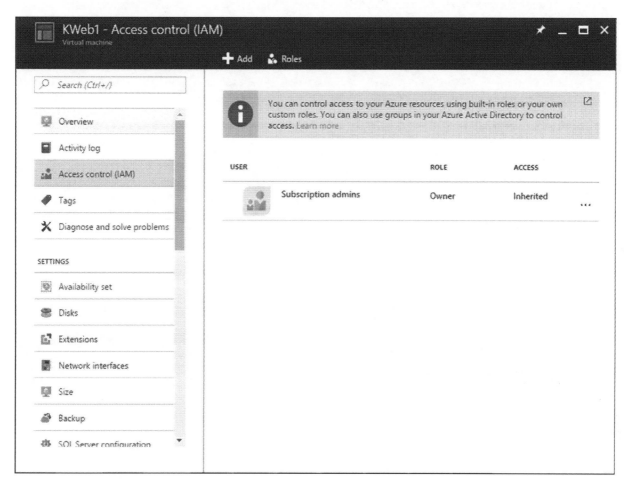

2. Click +Add. In Select a Role, select contributor. In Add users select webadmin1. Click Select and click ok.

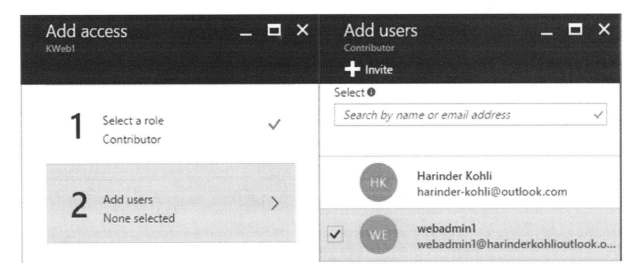

3. Log on to https://portal.azure.com with webadmin1@harinderkohlioutlook.onmicrosoft.com

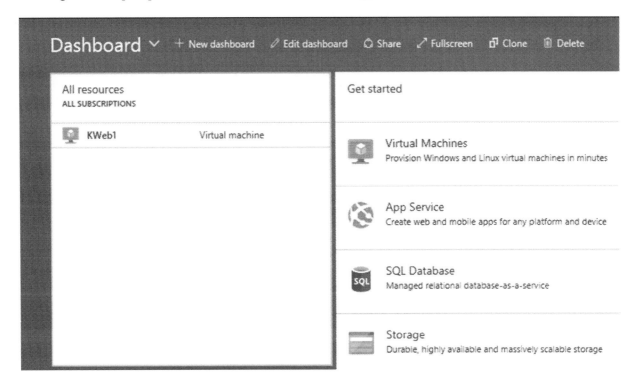

4. Webadmin1 can manage only KWeb1 VM
5. Click + New. You will find no options to add a resource.

Lab 19: Creating 2 Users in AAD for managing Storage Account kstorgps1

1. **https://manage.windowsazure.com/** (Classic Portal).
2. Go to Default directory and click Manage Access.

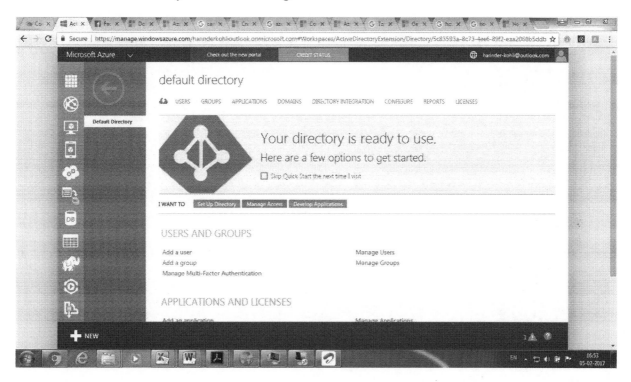

3. Click Add users.
4. Add 2 users storadmin1 and storadmin2.
5. The method is similar to webadmin1 user.I leave this as an exercise for the readers.

Lab 20: Create group and add storadmin1 and storadmin2

1. **https://manage.windowsazure.com/** (Classic Portal)
2. Go to Default directory and click Manage Access.

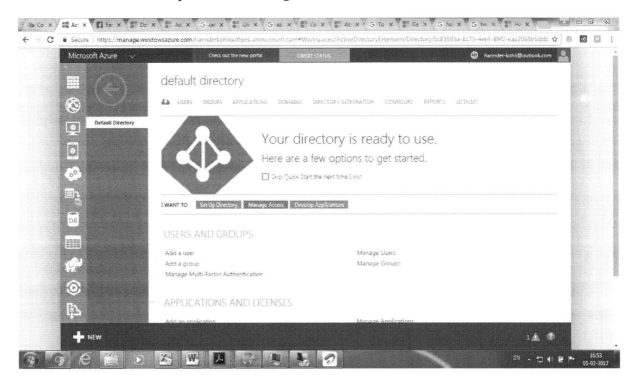

3. Click Add a group. Add group blade opens. Enter following information:

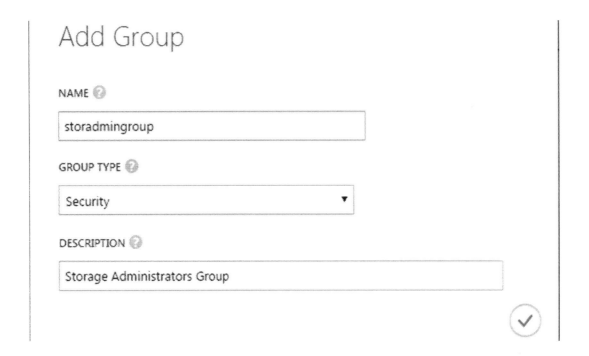

4. Go back to default directory>Manage Access.>Click Manage Groups
5. Click storadmingroup>Click Add Members
6. Add Member Blade opens> click storadmin1>click storadmin2.

Lab 21: Adding storadmin1 & storadmin2 to Storage Group kstorgps1

Note: Instead of adding users individually we will add storadmingroup group to Storage Group kstorgps1 and both the users will added to kstorgps1. **This is the advantage of creating groups.**

1. Go to Storage group kstorgps1 pane and click Access control (IAM)

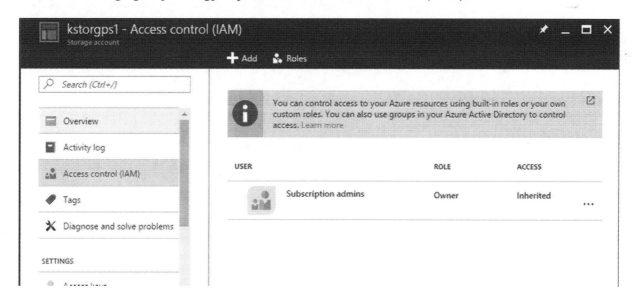

2. Click +Add>In Select a Role select contributor>In Add users select storadmingroup group> Click Select and click ok.

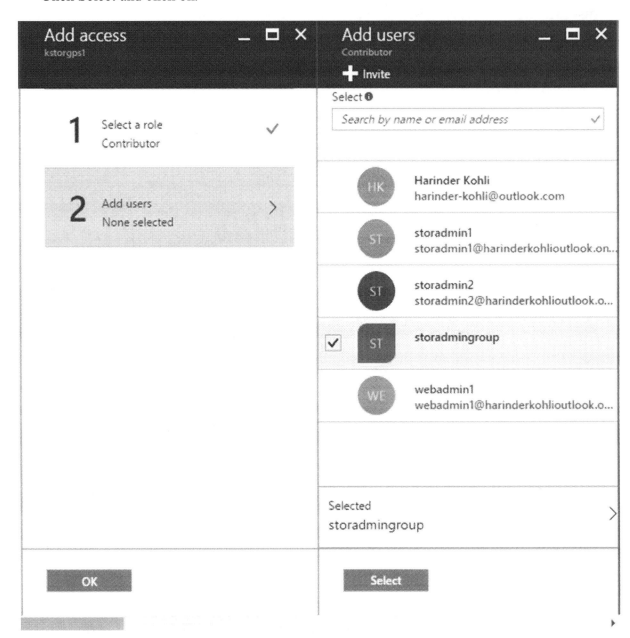

3. Log on https://portal.azure.com with storadmin1@harinderkohlioutlook.onmicrosoft.com

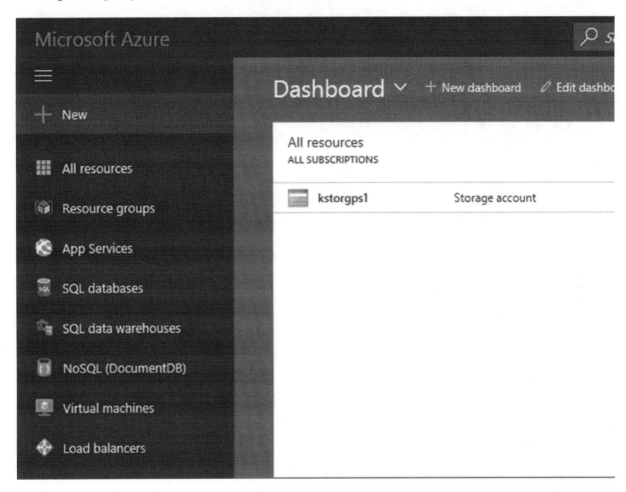

4. storadmin1 can only manage Storage Account kstorgps1.

Lab 22: Single Sign-on for SaaS Applications (Twitter)

1. **https://manage.windowsazure.com/** (Classic Portal)
2. Go to default Directory>Manage Access

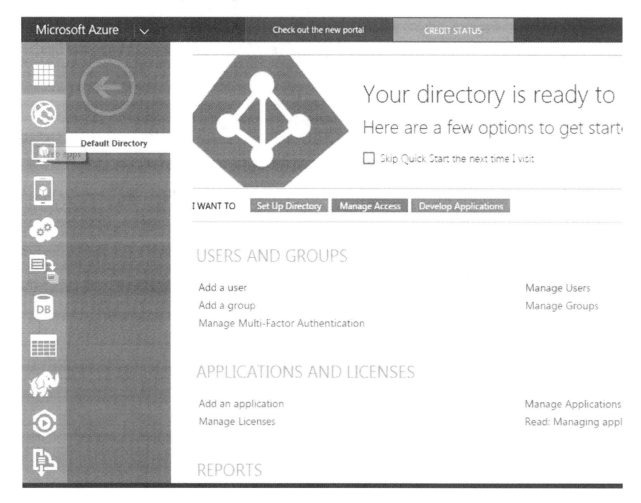

3. Click Add and application> Add and application Panel opens

4. In Add and application panel> type twitter in search box and enter. Twitter app come in application pane>Click the Twitter app and enter your twitter display name in Display Name box.>Click check mark.

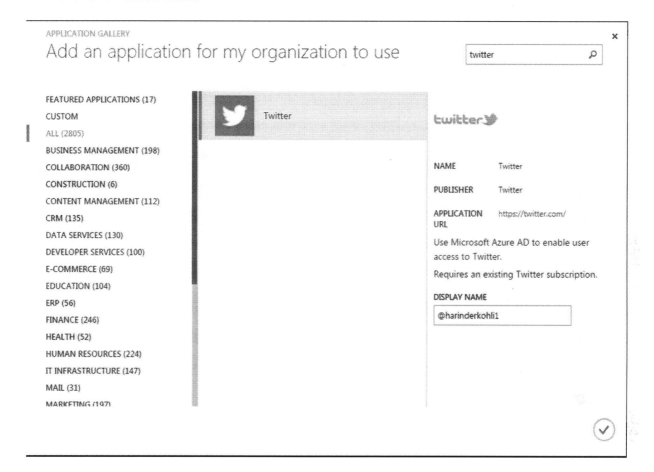

5. Click Configure single-sign-on>Select Password Single sign-on

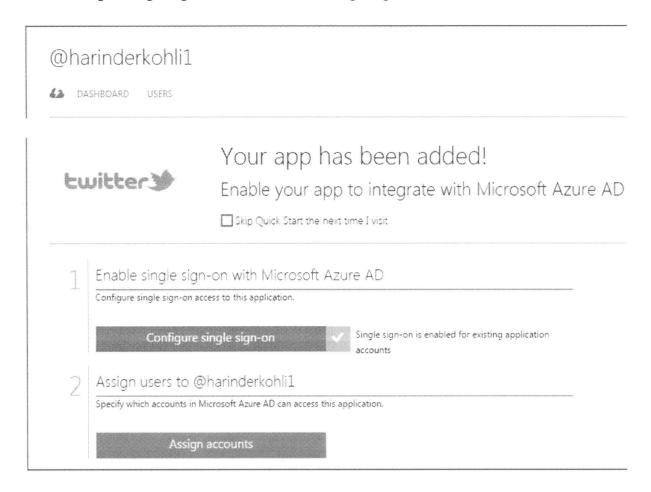

6. Click Assign Accounts>In this case I selected Harinder Kohli>Click Assign in the bottom pane.

@harinderkohli1

DISPLAY NAME	USER NAME	JOB TITLE	DEPARTMENT	ACCESS	METHOD	
Harinder Kohli	harinder-kohli@outlook.com			No	Unassigned	
storadmin1	storadmin1@harinderkohli...			No	Unassigned	
storadmin2	storadmin2@harinderkohli...			No	Unassigned	
webadmin1	webadmin1@harinderkohli...			No	Unassigned	

ASSIGN   EDIT ACCOUNT   REMOVE

7. Enter your Twitter email username and password and click check mark.

Assign Users

This action will allow the selected user to authenticate to the @harinderkohli1 application from within the Access Panel. Users can enter and update their @harinderkohli1 credentials using the Access Panel at any time.

☑ I want to enter @harinderkohli1 credentials on behalf of the user. Read deployment guidance.

User Name

xxxx@hotmail.com

Password

••••••••••••••

8. You get confirmation that twitter app is successfully added.

9. **https://account.activedirectory.windowsazure.com/**. This is your application access panel.

10. Click on Twitter App in application panel. Your Twitter account opens.

Chapter 7 - Azure Backup

Azure Backup is Backup as a service (BaaS) which you can use to backup and restore your data in Azure cloud.
You can backup both on Prem workloads and Azure workloads.
Azure Backups are stored in Recovery Services Vault.
Advantage of Azure backup is that we don t have to set up Backup infrastructure.

In this chapter we will add Recovery Vault and Backup Service to the topology. KWeb1-Backup VM will be created by restoring the backup of KWeb1 VM.

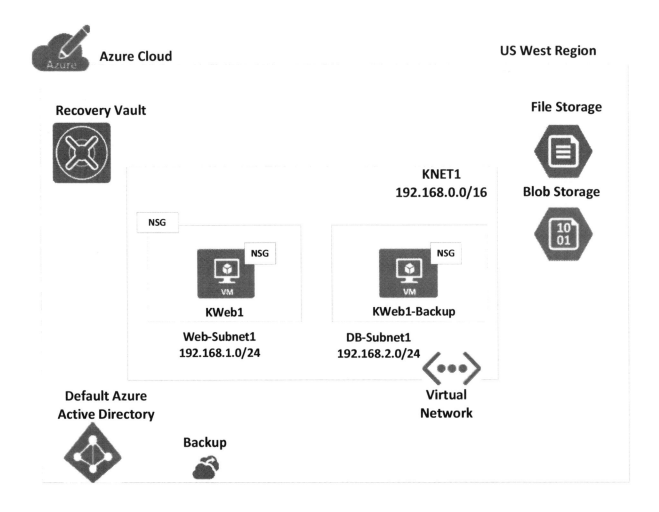

We will create following in the Backup labs:

1. Recovery Service vault.
2. Take backup of KWeb1 VM.
3. Restore backup of KWeb1 as VM KWeb1-Backup in DB-Subnet1.
4. Take backup of files and folders of on Premises Windows Server.

Lab 23: Create Recovery Services Vault

1. **https://portal.azure.com**
2. Click +New. In search box type Recovery Services and press enter.
3. In search result choose and click Backup and Site recovery (OMS).
4. Click create> In Recovery service Vault Blade enter following and click create.

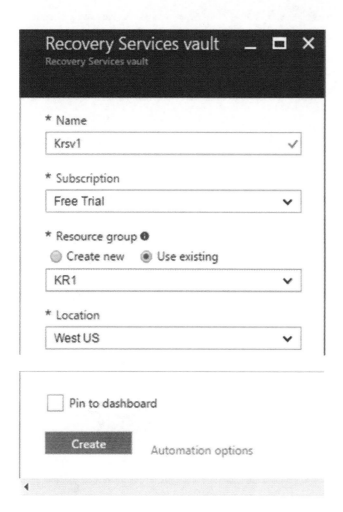

Lab 24: Setup Storage Redundancy to Locally-Redundant to save cost

1. Go Recovery services vault Krsv1 pane.
2. Click Backup Infrastructure>Backup Configuration> Locally-redundant>save

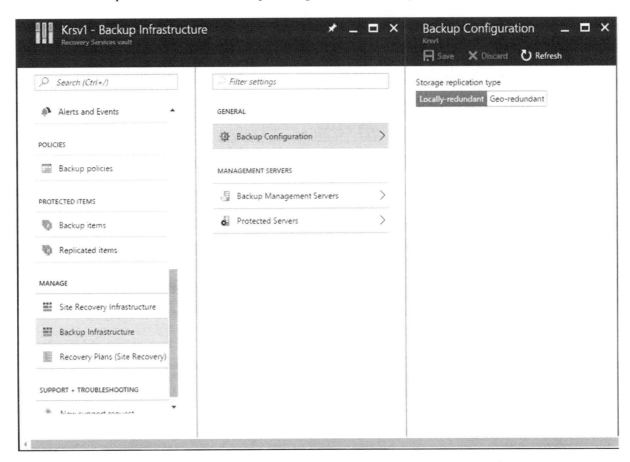

Lab 25: Backing Azure Workload KWeb1

1. Go Recovery services vault Krsv1 pane.
2. Click +Backup and select backup goal and select following and click ok.

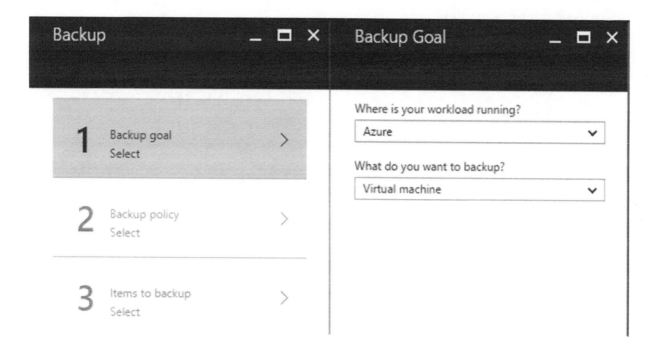

3. In Backup Policy select default Policy and click Ok>: Backup will happen daily at 5.30 PM.

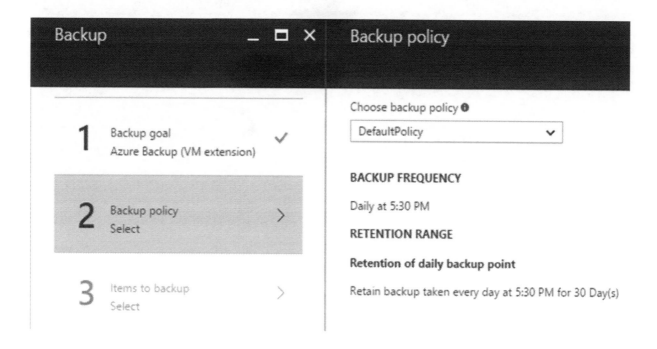

4. In items to backup select KWeb1 VM and click ok and then click enable backup.

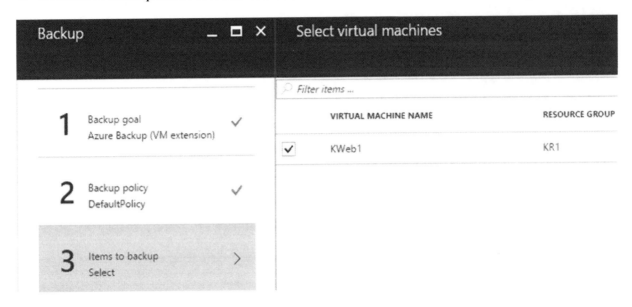

Important Note: Result of above action
Azure Backup service installs the backup extension to the VM Agent. The Azure Backup service seamlessly upgrades and patches the backup extension.

5. Check the Recovery Service vault Krsv1 pane if Backup job is listed or not

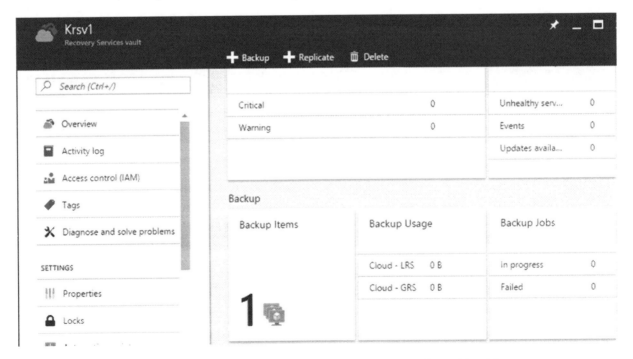

Note: It lists the item but the job is not progress as it is scheduled for 5.30 PM.

Lab 26: Triggering the backup job for KWeb1 VM for initial backup

1. Go to Recovery Service Vault Krsv1 dashboard and click backup item.

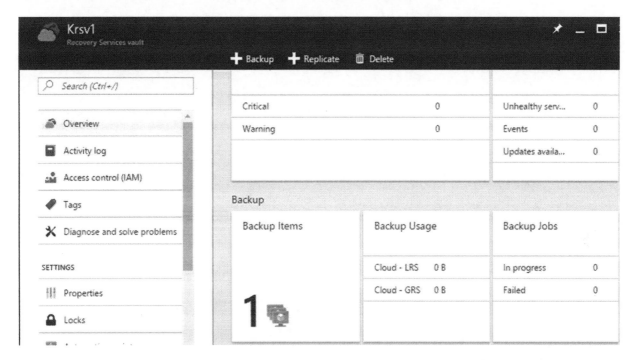

2. Select Backup Management type as Azure Virtual Machine. Select backup item kweb1.

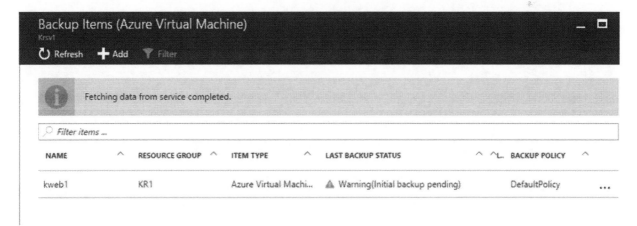

3. Click backup now and then click backup.

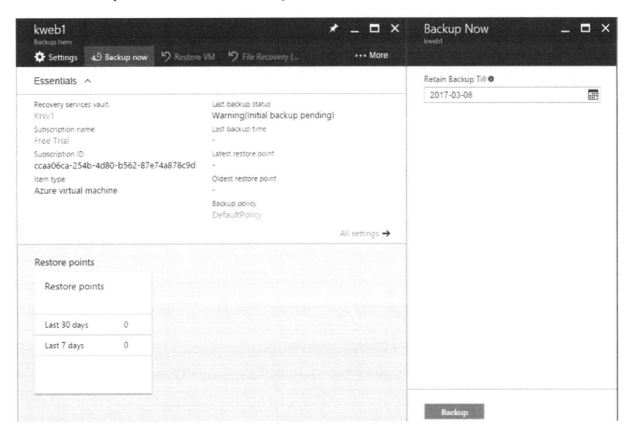

4. Monitor the backup job by clicking jobs under Monitoring and Reports on vault dashboard.

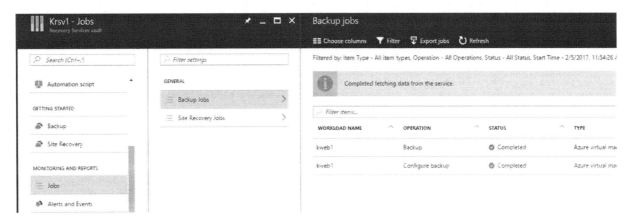

Lab 27: Restoring

1. In this lab we will restore KWeb1 VM for which we had configured backup in earlier lab.
2. Go Recovery services vault Krsv1 pane>Click Backup Tile>In backup management type click Azure Virtual Machine>Select KWeb1 VM>Backup Item KWeb1 pane opens.

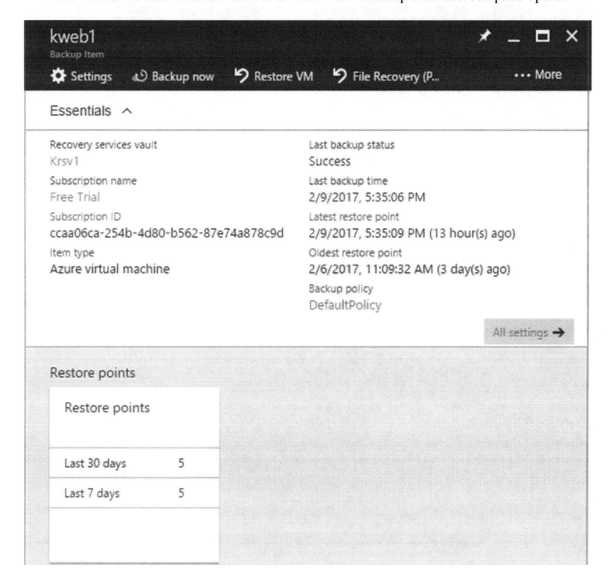

3. Click Restore VM>Select Restore Point blade opens>select a Restore and click ok and then restore.

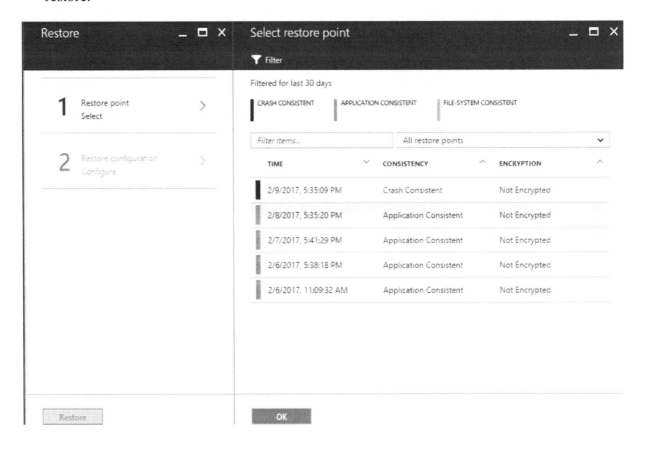

4. Restore Configuration Blade opens>specify following and click ok and then click restore. Note Restore type can be Create new virtual Machine or restore disk. In this lab we will restore Virtual machine in DB-Subnet1.

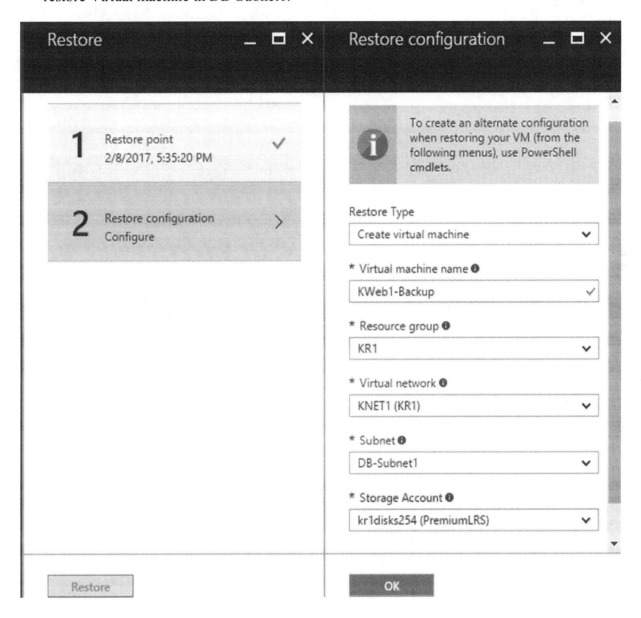

5. You monitor restore job in backup job pane. Restore is in progress.

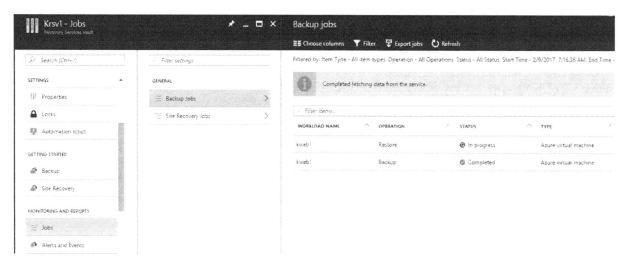

6. Restore job is completed. It took around 27 minutes to complete the job.

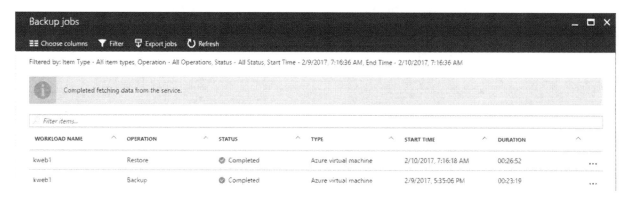

7. Click All Resources>Select KWeb1-Backup> KWeb1-Backup VM Dashboard opens.

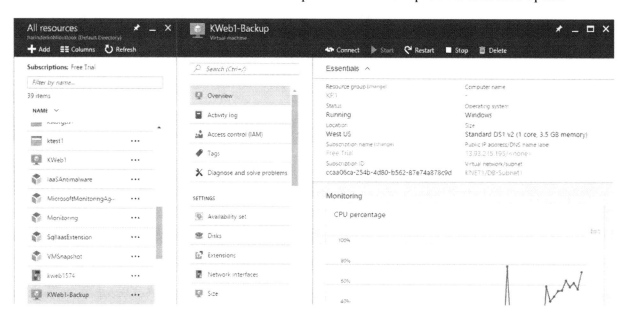

8. Lets check if default website works or not. In the dashboard Copy the IP 13.93.215.195 and open in browser. It works.

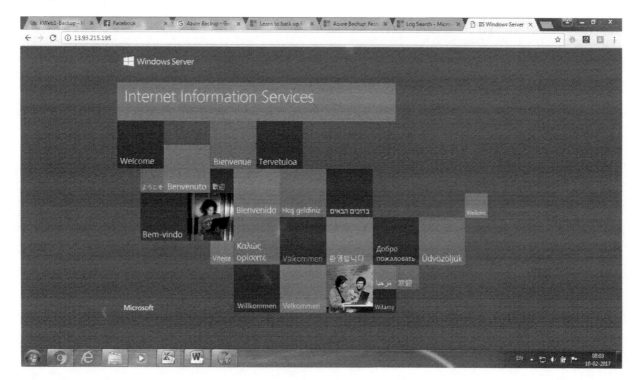

Lab 28: Backing On Prem Windows Workload

1. We will backup files and Folders from Windows 7 Professional 64 Bit desktop to Azure.
2. Go Recovery services vault Krsv1 pane.
3. Click +Backup> specify following> Click Infrastructure for backup to Azure.

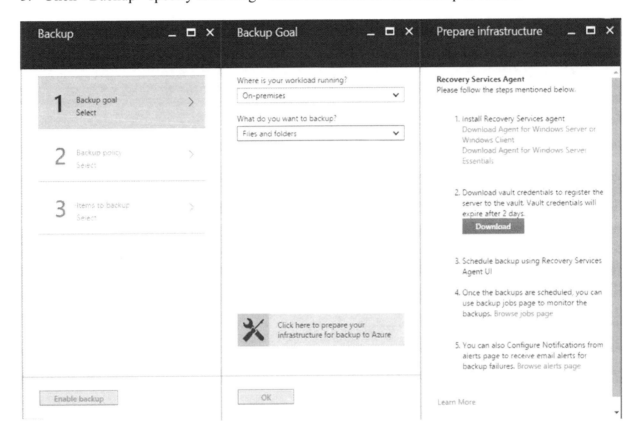

4. Click Download Agent for windows server>It will download MARSAgentInstaller.exe on the desktop.
5. Download Vault Credentials. Vault Credentials are required to register the server to the Recovery Services Vault.

6. On the windows 7 on prem desktop double click MARSAgentInstaller.exe and start installation of the agent. At the end of installation click Proceed to Registration to register your on prem windows 7 desktop to Recovery Services Vault.

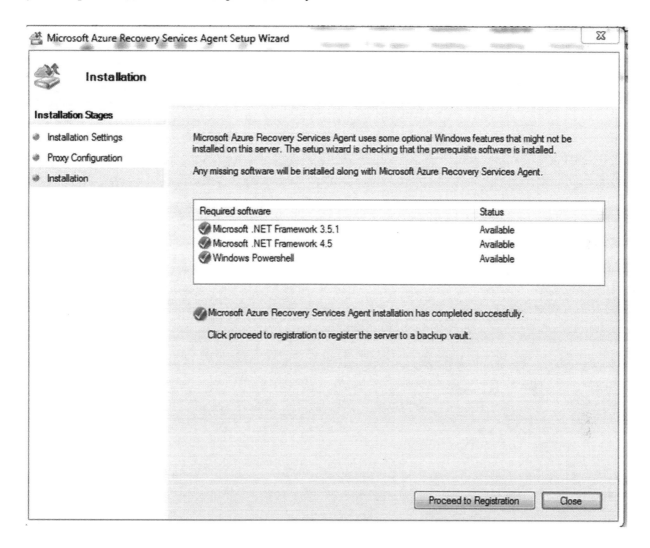

7. Browse and attach Vault credentials file downloaded earlier.

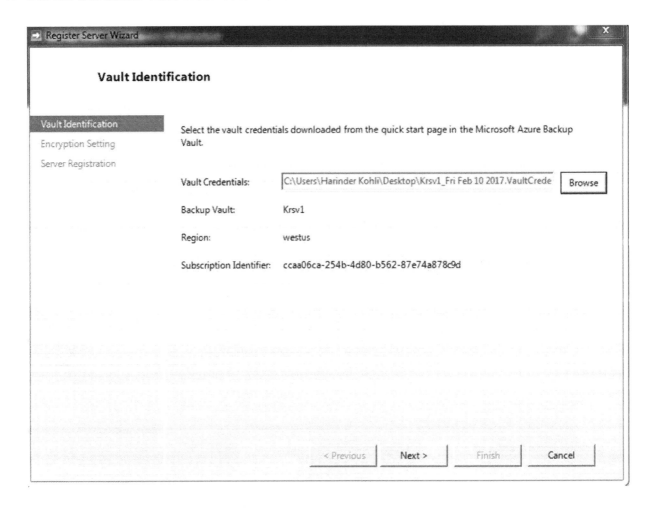

8. In Encryption setting specify following> Click finish.

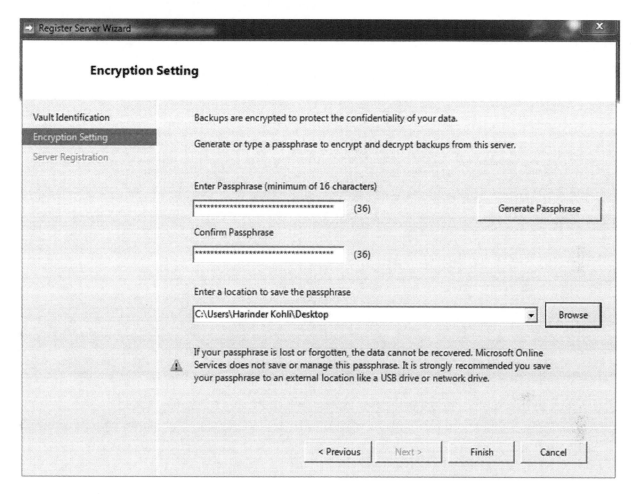

9. I have created a TestBackup Folder in C drive. In my TestBackup folder I have created TestBackup.txt file. We will backup this file to Azure.

10. Open Microsoft Azure Backup agent on windows 7 desktop to Schedule backup>Click Action>Click Schedule Backup>Schedule Backup Wizard open>In Select Items to backup select TestBackup.txt file and for rest select all default values> Click close.

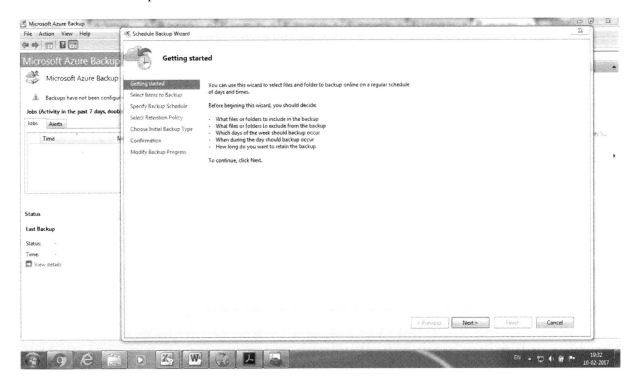

11. To back up files and folders for the first time>Go To Microsoft Azure Backup Agent>Action>Backup now>On confirmation page click back up>Click close>Monitor the progress in agent console. Once the job is completed go to Recovery Services Vault in Azure.

12. Go Recovery services vault Ksrv1>Click Backup Items.

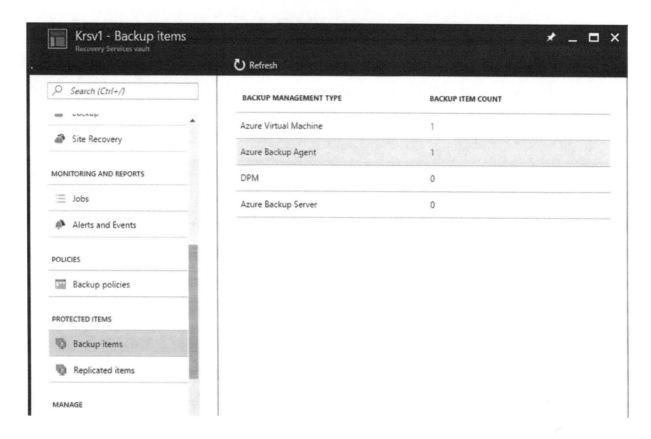

13. Click Azure Backup Agent. You can see Under backup item C:\ on harinderkohli

Chapter 8 - Azure SQL Database

Azure SQL Database is a relational database-as-a-service in the cloud built on the Microsoft SQL Server.
The benefit of using the Azure SQL Database service is the ability to spin up and consume a relational database in minutes; it can then easily be replicated for geo redundancy without all the infrastructure deployment and management normally required.

SQL databases is available in Basic, Standard, and Premium service tiers. Each service tier offers different levels of performance and capabilities to support lightweight to heavyweight database workloads.

Each tier is distinguished primarily by performance, which is measured in Database Transaction/Throughput Units (DTUs). There are Multiple Performace levels within a Tier.

In this chapter we will add Azure SQL Database Service to the topology

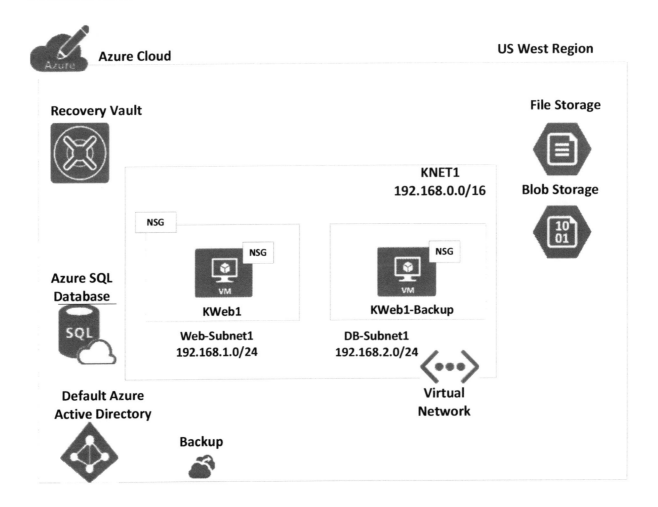

This Topology will be used in Lab 33

US West

US East

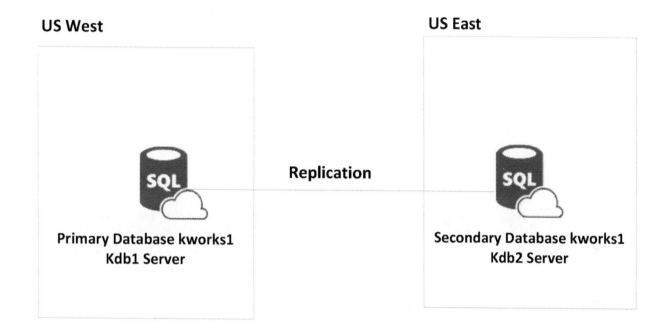

Replication

Primary Database kworks1
Kdb1 Server

Secondary Database kworks1
Kdb2 Server

We will create following in Azure SQL Database Lab:

1. SQL Database Kworks1.
2. Access Kworks1 using SSMS which is already installed on KWeb1 VM.
3. Create replica of kworks1 in US East region.
4. Restore kworks1 from replica back to US West region.

Lab 29: Deploying Azure SQL Database

1. **https://portal.azure.com**
2. Click +New>Databases>SQL Database. In the SQL Database blade enter following. Pricing tier is Basic. Click select than create.

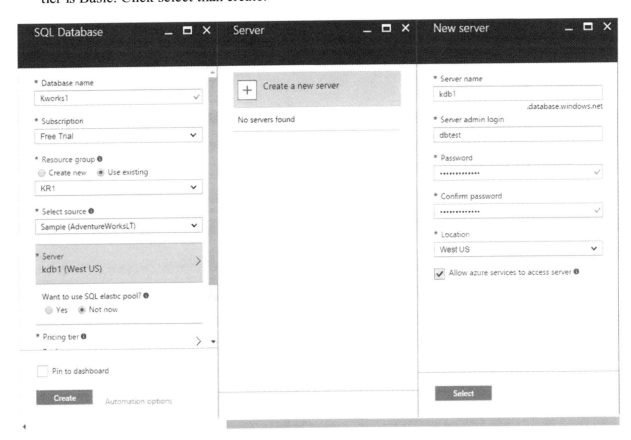

Lab 30: Configuring Server firewall to allow SQL Database connectivity from KWeb1 VM

1. If you stop KWeb1 VM, you need to update the firewall rules to account for the change of IP address.
2. Note down the IP Address of KWeb1 VM. It is 13.64.247.139.
3. Go the SQL Database Kworks1 Pane.

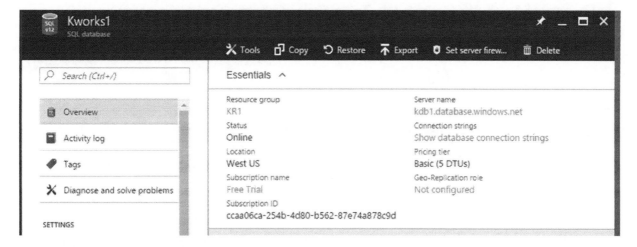

4. Click Set server firewall and enter KWeb1 VM IP and click save.

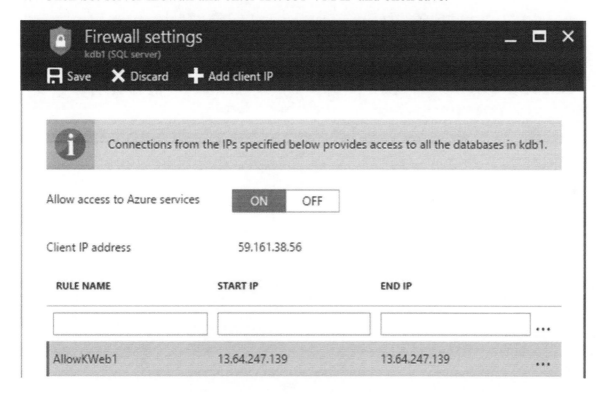

Lab 31: Connecting to Azure SQL database from KWeb1 VM

1. From your desktop RDP to KWeb1 VM.
2. Start SQL Server 2016 Management Studio (SSMS).
3. In Connect to Server dialog box, specify the following settings, and then click Connect.

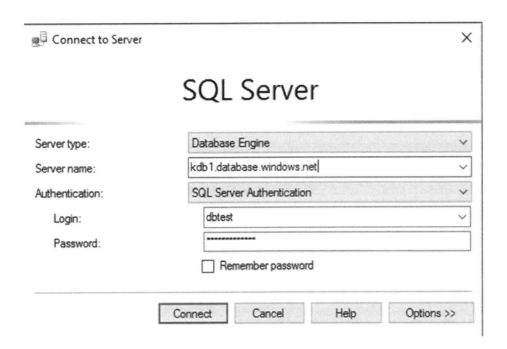

4. In SQL Server Management Studio, in Object Explorer, under the server name, expand Databases, and you can see that the Kworks1 database is listed.

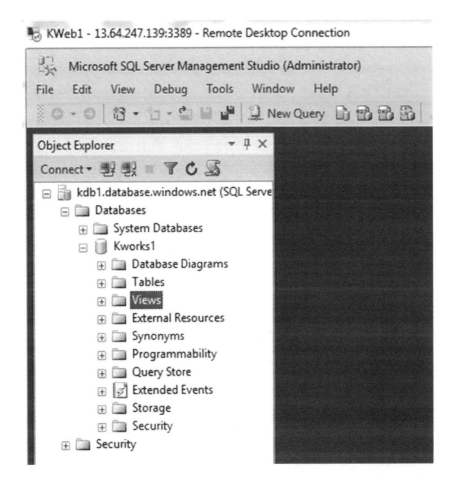

Lab 32: Creating Replica of Kworks1 Database using Geo-Replication

Geo Replication will create a replica database in the region you specify. In our case primary database Kworks1 is in US West Region. We will create replica database in US East Region.

1. Go the SQL Database Kworks1 Pane.
2. Select Geo replication>Select US East Region in Map>create Secondary blade opens. Specify the following settings in create Secondary Blade and click select and then ok.

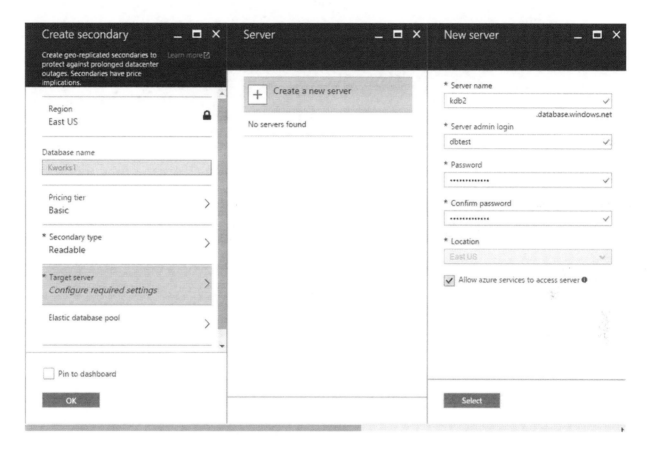

3. It will take around 2 minutes for deployment to complete.
4. In SQL Database Kworks1 Pane. Click Geo-Replication>Select Secondaries>secondary Database Pane opens.

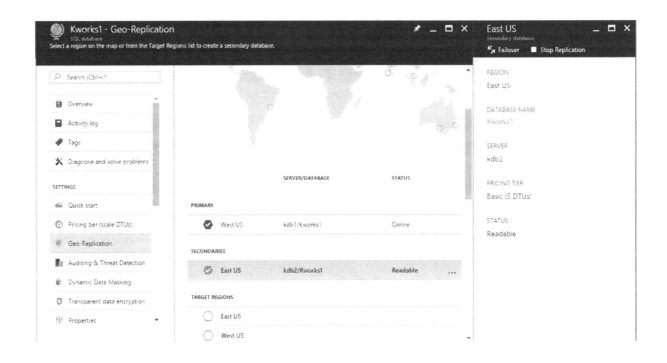

Note the Failover and Stop Replication option in Secondary Database.

Lab 33: Restore an Azure SQL Database from a geo-redundant backup

1. I will leave this an exercise for the readers but will give a hint.
2. **https://portal.azure.com**
3. Click +New>Databases>SQL Database. In the SQL Database blade enter following.

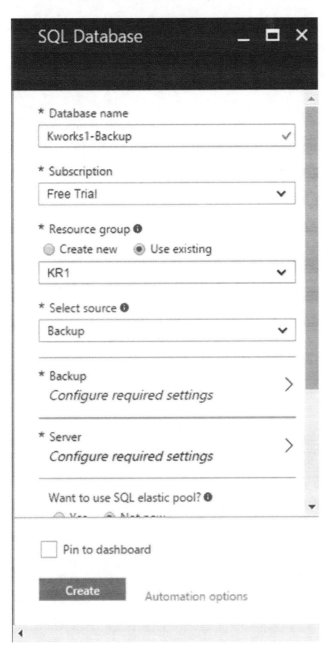

4. In Backup select replica database Kworks1 and kdb2 server in US East.
5. In Server where restore will happen select kdb1 which is US West.

Chapter 9 - Azure Security Center

Azure Security Center is an Azure service that helps you prevent, detect, and respond to threats against your Azure resources. It helps detect threats that might otherwise go unnoticed, and works with a broad ecosystem of security solutions.

Azure Security Center can be used to monitor your infrastructure as a service (IaaS) resources, such as Azure Virtual Machines and Azure Virtual Network, in addition to PaaS resources such as Azure SQL Database.

Azure Security Center uses global threat intelligence from Microsoft products and services, the Microsoft Digital Crimes Unit (DCU), the Microsoft Security Response Center (MSRC), and external feeds. For detection purposes, it also applies advanced analytics, including machine learning and behavioral analysis.

In this chapter we will add Azure Security Center service to the topology

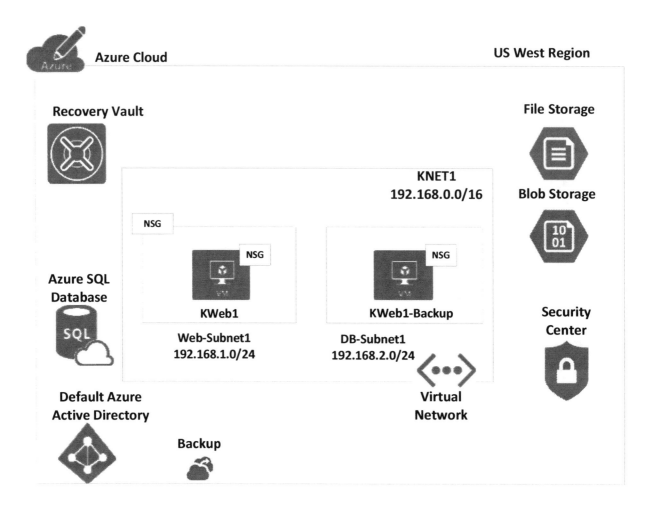

We will create following in Security Service Lab:

1. Enable Security Centre and upgrade to Standard Free Trial.
2. Remediate By Enabling Encryption for Azure Storage Account.
3. Remediate by Providing Security Contact Details.
4. Remediate by Installing Endpoint Protection on Kweb1 VM

Lab 34: Enable Azure Security Center

1. https://portal.azure.com
2. In the left pane, click Security Center. Click Launch Security Center.

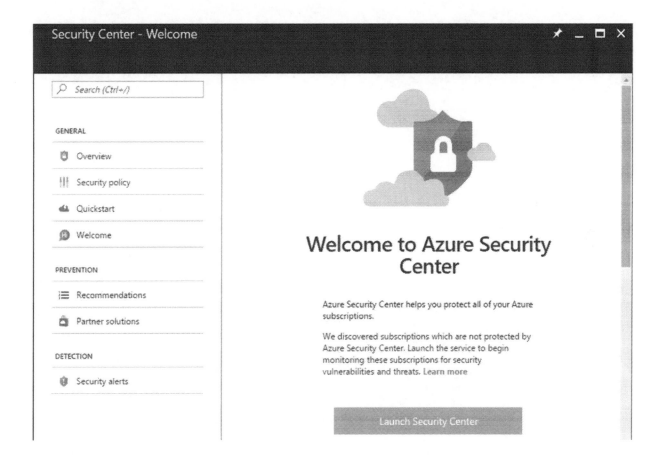

3. Security Center Dashboard Opens.

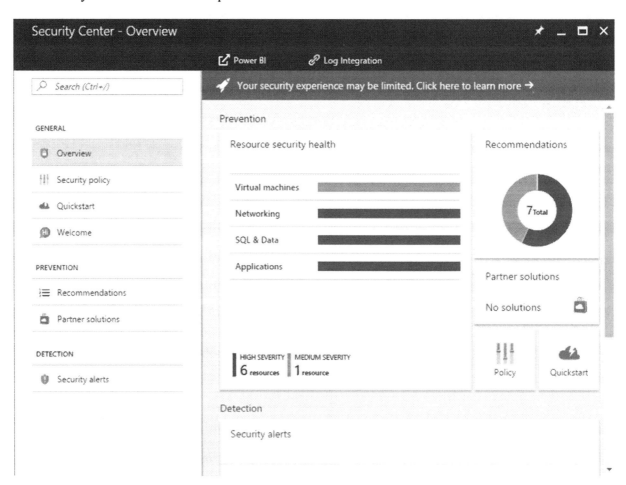

Lab 35: Status of Security Components and upgrade to Standard free Trial

Note 1: In this lab we will check status of Data Collection & Prevention policy components, Specify Email Details and upgrade to Standard Free Trial.
Note 2: By default Data Collection is on and Prevention policy components are on. If not on enable them by going to Security Policy.

1. Security Center Dashboard>Click Security Policy in Left pane>Click free trial. Data Collection is on.

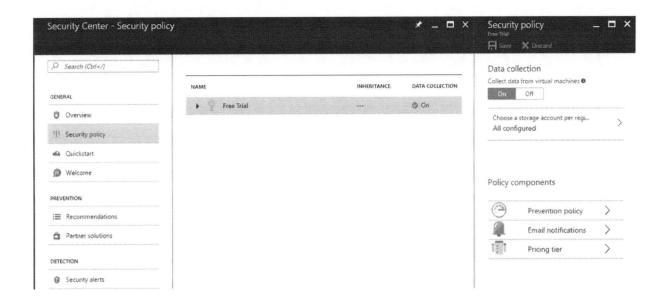

2. Click Prevention Policy. By default all Components are on. Click Ok.

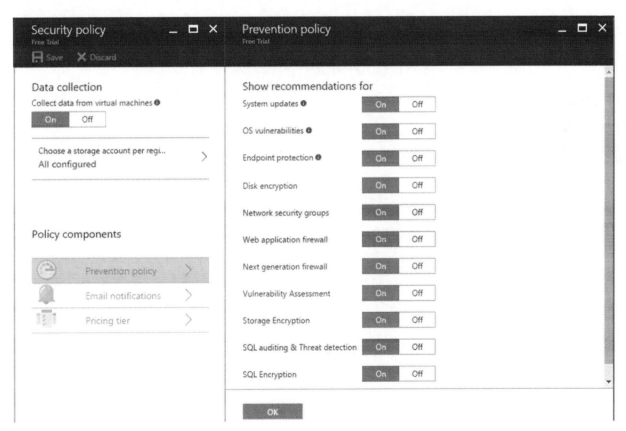

3. Click Email Notification. click ok. We will specify this information later.

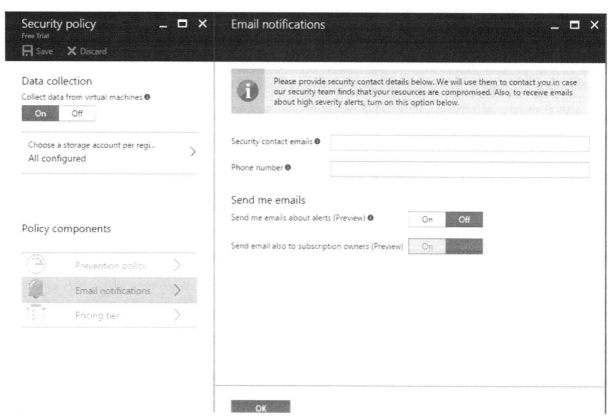

4. Click Pricing Tier> Select Standard Free Trial.>Click select>Click Save.

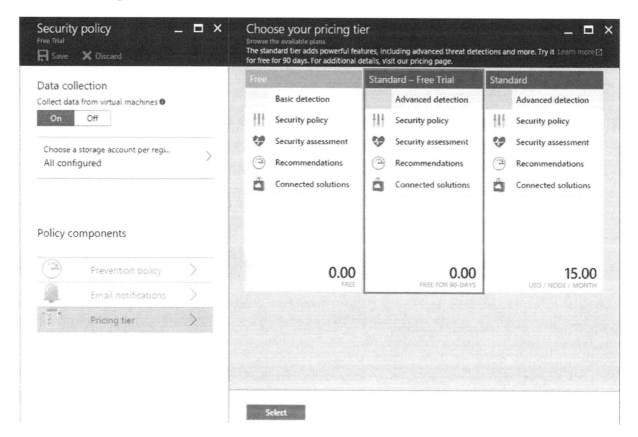

Lab 36: Checking various options in Security Center Dashboard

1. Click Recommendation in Security Center Dashboard.

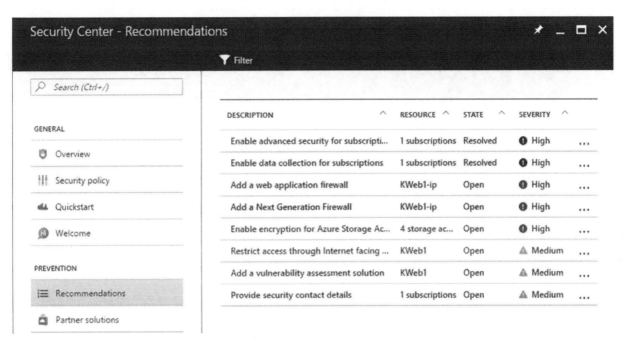

Note 1: It is giving recommendation to add firewall and vulnerability assessment solution to Web1 VM.

Note 2: It is giving recommendation to add security contact details for subscription.

2. Click Security alerts in Security Center Dashboard to check alerts.

3. In Security Center Dashboard, under Resource security health click Virtual Machines, Networking, SQL & Data and Applications.

Lab 37: Remediate By Enabling Encryption for Azure Storage Account

1. Security Center Dashboard >Click Recommendation in Security Center Dashboard.You can see there are 4 Storage Accounts where encryption is not enabled.

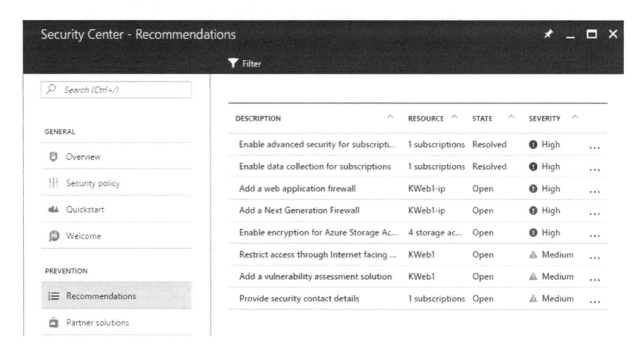

2. Click Enable Encryption for Azure Storage Account in Recommendation blade>Enable Storage encryption blade opens>select Storage Account Kstorgps1>Click Enabled> Click save.

3. Refresh your browser with f5. Go to Recommendation. You can see now there are 3 Storage accounts where encryption is not enabled instead of 4 earlier.

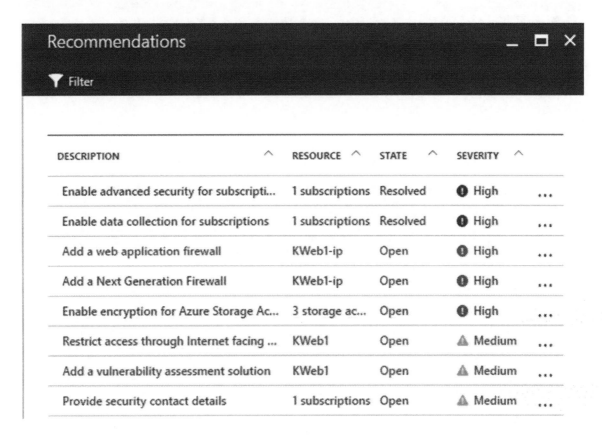

Lab 38: Remediate by Providing Security Contact Details

1. Security Center Dashboard >Click Recommendation in Security Center Dashboard. You can see Security Contact Details for subscription are missing.

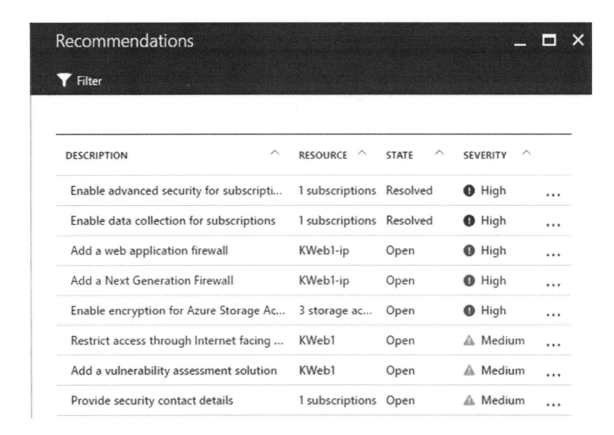

2. Click Provide security contact details>Click Subscription Free trial>Provide Security detail blade open>specify following and click on.

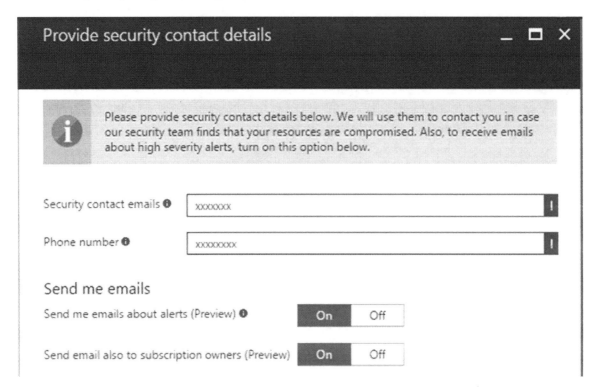

Note: See the progress in the security contact details. It will turn from progress to resolved.

3. Go to Recommendation. Provide security contact details issue is resolved (last row).

Recommendations _ ▢ ✕

▼ Filter

DESCRIPTION ⌃	RESOURCE ⌃	STATE ⌃	SEVERITY ⌃	
Enable advanced security for subscripti...	1 subscriptions	Resolved	❗ High	...
Enable data collection for subscriptions	1 subscriptions	Resolved	❗ High	...
Install Endpoint Protection	KWeb1	Open	❗ High	...
Add a web application firewall	KWeb1-ip	Open	❗ High	...
Add a Next Generation Firewall	KWeb1-ip	Open	❗ High	...
Enable encryption for Azure Storage Ac...	3 storage ac...	Open	❗ High	...
Restrict access through Internet facing ...	KWeb1	Open	⚠ Medium	...
Add a vulnerability assessment solution	KWeb1	Open	⚠ Medium	...
Provide security contact details	1 subscriptions	Resolved	⚠ Medium	...

Lab 39: Remediate by Installing Endpoint Protection on Kweb1 VM

1. Security Center Dashboard >Click Recommendation in Security Center Dashboard. You can see there is Recommendation to Install Endpoint Protection on KWeb1 VM.

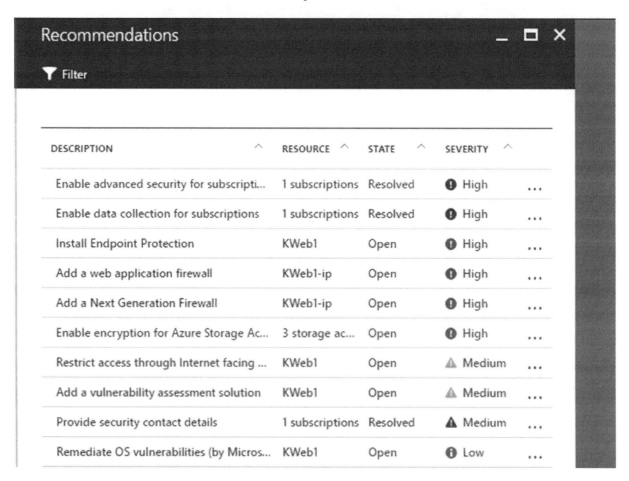

2. In Recommendation Blade>Click Install Endpoint Protection>Install Endpoint protection Blade opens>Click VM KWeb1>select endpoint protection blade opens>select Microsoft Antimalware>click create

3. In install MS Antimalware Blade >Select default values and click ok.

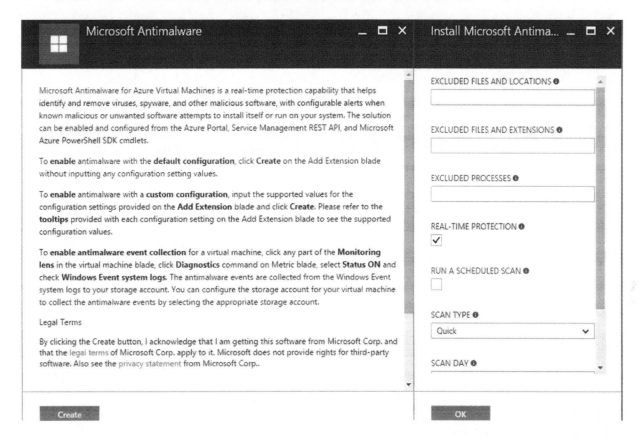

4. Go back to recommendations blade and you will see the issue resolved.

Lab 40: Remediate by adding a vulnerability assessment solution

1. Click Recommendation in Security Center Dashboard.
2. Click Recommendation Add a vulnerability assessment solution>Add a vulnerability assessment solution bladeopens>Select Kweb1 VM and click install.

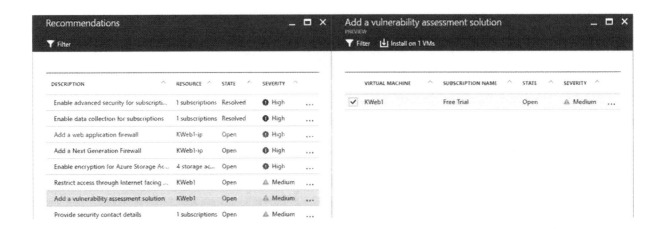

3. Click create new. Create a new vulnerability assessment solution blade opens. Click Qyalys.

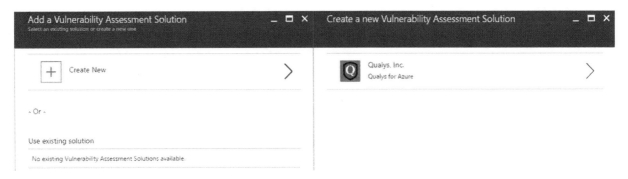

4. Qualys blade opens. Specify following and click ok.you need to get license code from Qyalys.

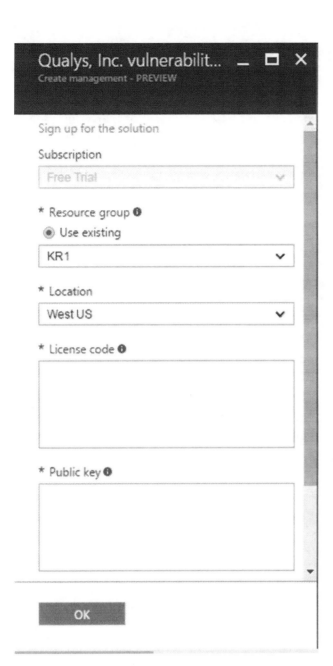

Chapter 10 - Microsoft Operations Management Suite

Operations Management Suite (OMS) is a collection of cloud-based services for managing your on-premises and cloud environments.

It Consist of Four cloud based services plus Management Solutions. Note these are individual services. You don t require one for other to function.
Log Analytics
Automation & Control
Protection and Disaster Recovery (Backup & ASR)
Security and Compliance
The common component in all four services is OMS repository which is hosted in Azure cloud.

Management solutions extend the functionality of Operations Management Suite (OMS) by providing packaged management scenarios that customers can add to their environment. Management solution packs have Pre Built rules and Algorithms that perform analysis. Management solutions can be installed from the Solutions Gallery in the OMS portal.

You can manage all four services and Management Solutions through OMS portal.
You can access OMS portal at **https://<OMS workspace name>.portal.mms.microsoft.com**

The advantage of OMS is that it is implemented as a cloud-based service, you can have it up and running quickly with minimal investment in infrastructure services. New features are delivered automatically, saving you on going maintenance and upgrade costs.

Log Analytics

Log Analytics is a service in Operations Management Suite (OMS) that helps you collect and analyze data generated by resources in your cloud and on-premises environments.

It gives you real-time insights using integrated search and custom dashboards to readily analyze millions of records across all of your workloads and servers regardless of their physical location.

At the center of Log Analytics is the OMS repository which is hosted in the Azure cloud. The combined solution is known as OMS Workspace. Data is collected into the repository from connected sources by configuring data sources and adding solutions to your subscription.

To Monitor on Prem Servers you require MS Monitoring Agent (MMA).
For Azure Virtual Machines you require Microsoft Monitoring Agent virtual machine extension.

In this chapter we will add OMS Repository, Log analytics Service, Security & Compliance Service and Management Solutions to the topology.

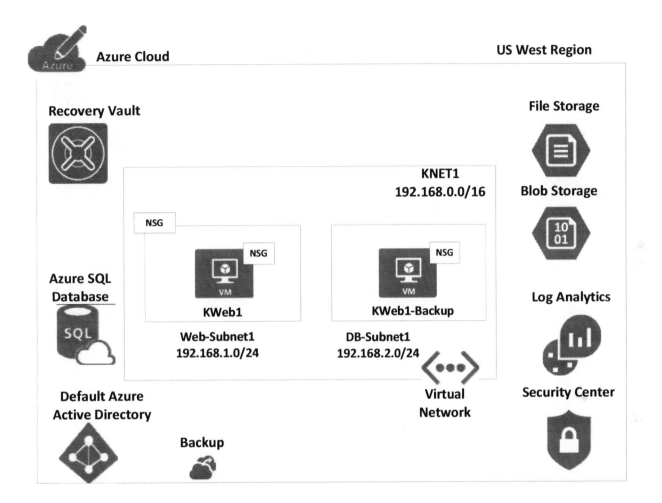

We will create following in OMS Lab:

1. Create OMS Workspace (It will add OMS Repository and Log Analytics Service)
2. Add Connected Sources
3. Add Data Sources
4. Add Security & Compliance Service
5. Add Management Solutions

Lab 41: Creating OMS workspace

1. https://portal.azure.com
2. Click + New > In the search box type Log Analytics>In the search results choose Log Analytics> Log Analytics create OMS workspace blade opens>Click create > OMS workspace blade opens>specify following and click ok.

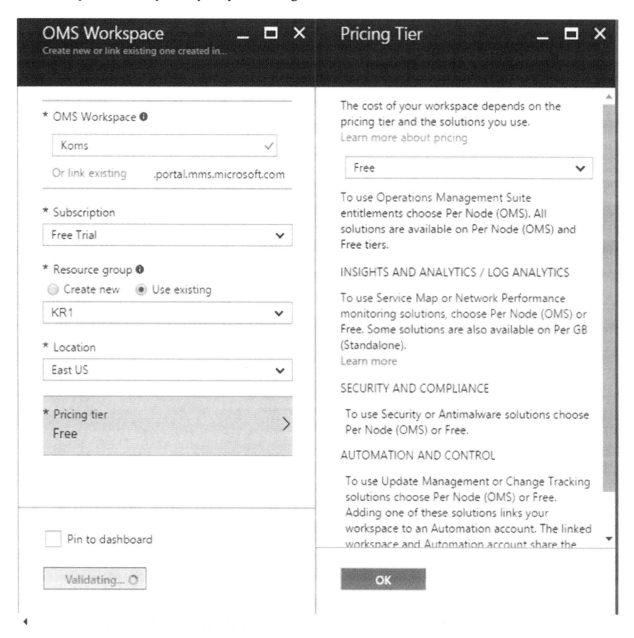

Lab 42: Add Connected Source - Azure Virtual Machines to Log Analytics

1. In this lab we will install Log Analytics agent through the Log Analytics VM extension
2. Go to log Analytics Dashboard Koms>Click Virtual Machines. It shows OMS Connection Not Connected.

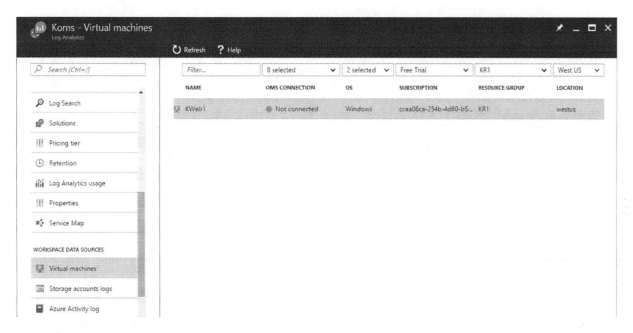

3. Click KWeb1 Virtual Machine> KWeb1 VM Blade opens> Click Connect

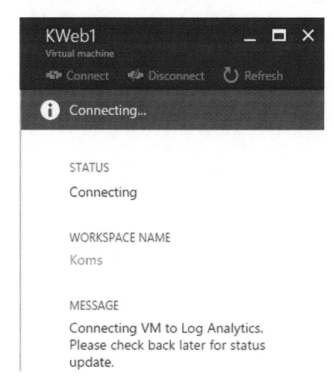

Lab 43: Add Connected Source - On Prem Windows Server to Log Analytics

1. In this lab we will install Microsoft Monitoring Agent (MMA) on my windows 7 Professional 64 bit desktop.
2. Log on to OMS portal either by going to https://koms.portal.mms.microsoft.com or by clicking OMS portal in Log Analytics Dashboard.

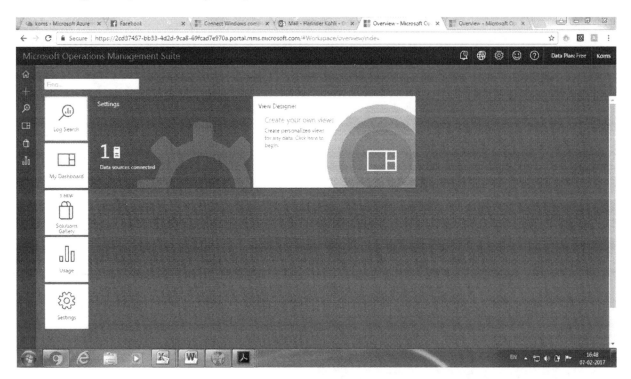

3. Click Setting>Connected sources>Windows Servers. Download Windows agent 64 bit exe file and **copy Workspace id and Primary Key in Notepad.**

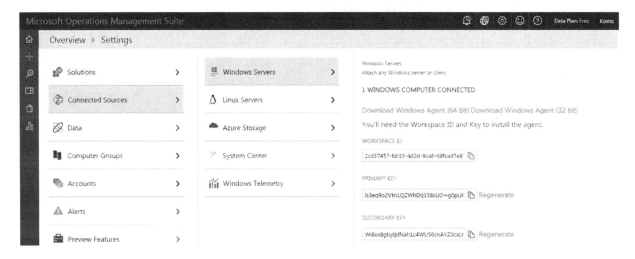

4. On windows 7 desktop click the MMA exe file. Specify following during installation.

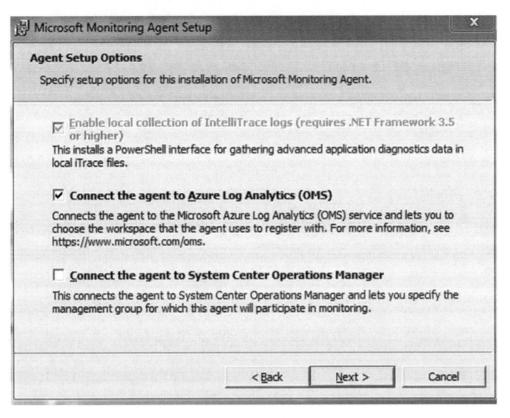

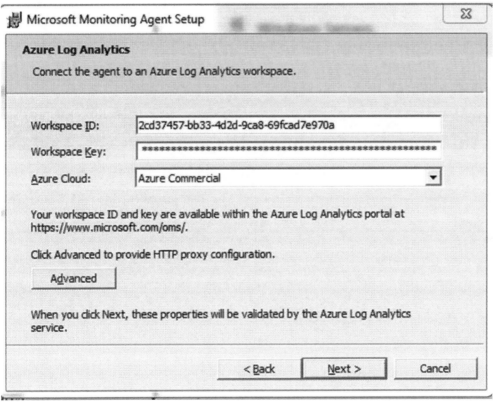

5. Go to OMS Portal>Settings>Connected Sources. You can see 1 Windows Computer connected. Click on it. You can see Windows 7 desktop Harinder Kohli and Azure VM KWeb1.

6. Click both computers and check for information and options available. You can also create alerts here.

Lab 44: Add Azure Storage Account kstorgps1

1. Go to log Analytics Dashboard Koms>Click Storage account logs>+Add.

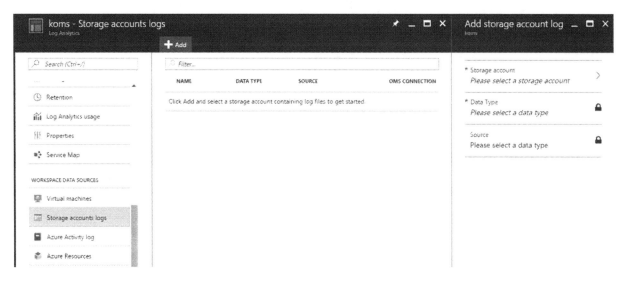

2. In Add Storage Account Log>Specify following and click ok.

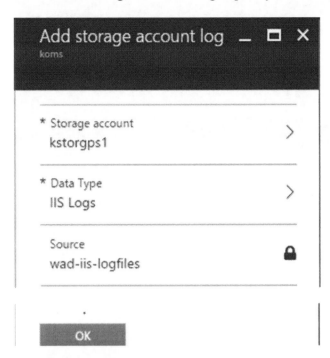

3. Repeat step 3 to add Events

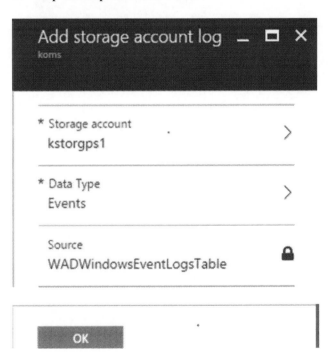

Lab 45: Add Azure Activity Log

1. Go to log Analytics Dashboard Koms>Click Azure Activity Log> Click free Trial under Subscription>Free Trial blade opens>Click Connect in top right.

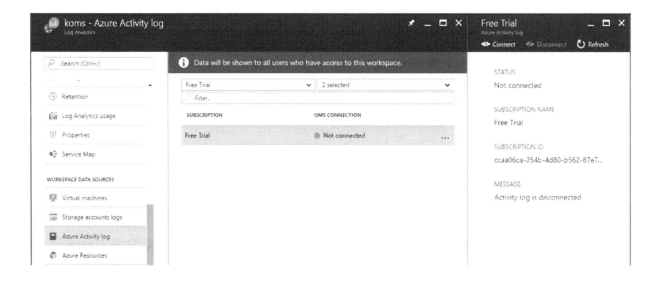

Lab 46: Add Data Source - Windows Event Logs

Log Analytics collects events from the Windows event logs that are specified in the settings. Yo can add an event log by typing in the name of the log and clicking + or Enter. For each log, only the events with the selected severities are collected. Check the severities for the particular log that you want to collect.

1. Log on to OMS portal either by going to **https://koms.portal.mms.microsoft.com** or by clicking OMS portal in Log Analytics Dashboard.
2. Click Setting>Data>Windows Event Logs> In the search box type event name and press enter. Make sure to click save in top left.
3. In below example I entered Application in search box and then press enter. Similarly you enter various events like HardwareEvents, Systems etc.
4. Hint: to look for name of the log to type in search box, You can go to event viewer in windows server.

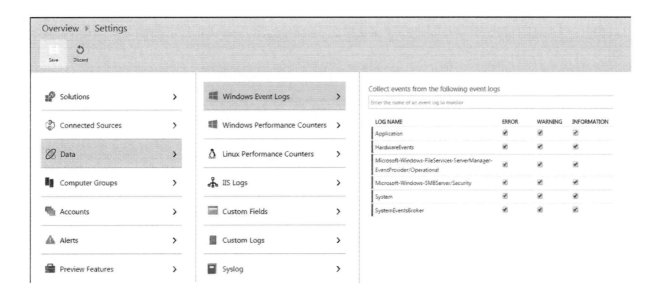

Lab 47: Add Data Source - IIS log

Internet Information Services (IIS) stores user activity in log files that can be collected by Log Analytics. Log Analytics only supports IIS log files stored in W3C format.

1. Log on to OMS portal by going to https://koms.portal.mms.microsoft.com
2. Click Setting>Data>IIS Logs>Select Collect W3C format IIS log files.

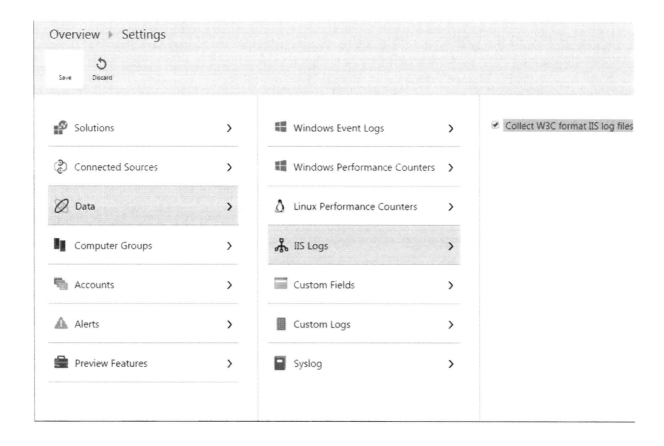

Lab 48: Add Data Source - Windows Performance Counters

Performance counters in Windows provide insight into the performance of hardware components, operating systems, and applications. Log Analytics can collect performance counters.

1. Log on to OMS portal either by going to **https://koms.portal.mms.microsoft.com** or by clicking OMS portal in Log Analytics Dashboard.
2. Click Setting>Data>Windows Performance Counters>Click Add the selected Performance counters or type the counter name in search field and press enter.

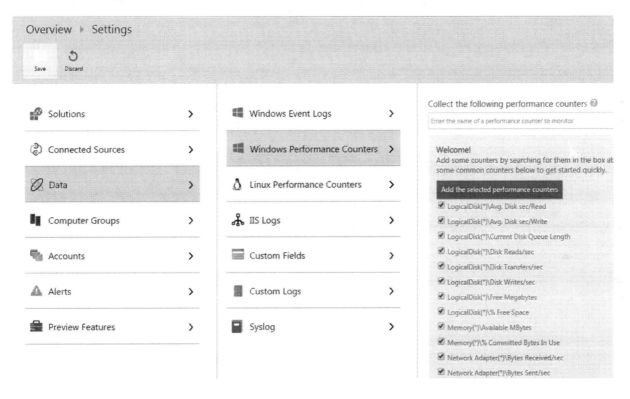

3. After clicking Add the selected Performance counters, following opens.

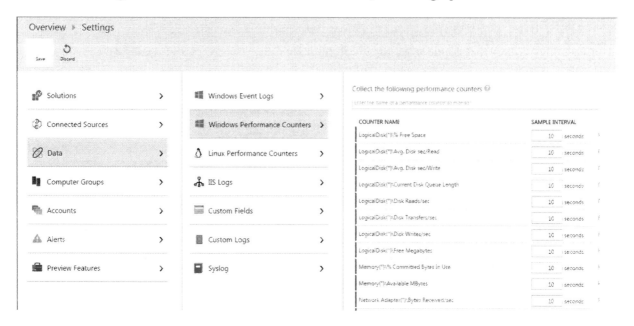

4. We will change the Sample interval to 1200 seconds to conserve storage space and cost. Click save to save the configuration.

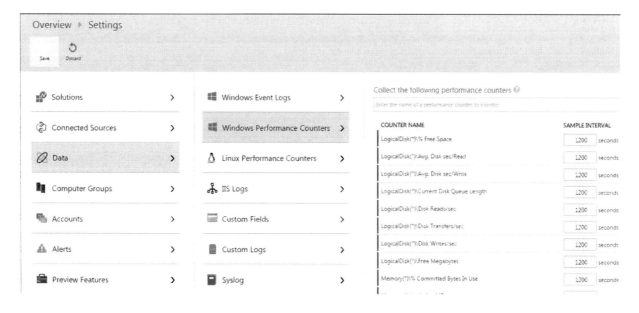

Lab 49: Query Log Data with Log Search

Log Search allows you to combine and correlate any data from multiple sources within your environment including On Prem and Cloud.

1. Log on to OMS portal to **https://koms.portal.mms.microsoft.com**
2. Click Log search in OMS Portal> Log search Blade opens.

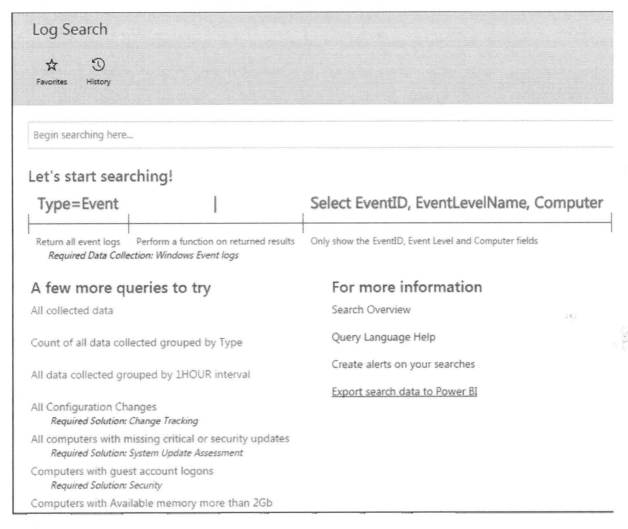

Query using Search Box: In search box you can search for an event or performance counter etc. On the Search box, you can create a query, and then when you search, you can filter the results by using facet controls. You can also create advanced queries to transform, filter, and report on your results.

Type=Perf. This will show only performance counter.

Type=Perf ObjectName=Processor. This will show counters related to processor only.

3. Click **All Collected Data** in Log Search Pane and you get following. On left pane you can see there are 6 types of data including Performance Counters, Events, IIS logs etc. On right pane there are results for all 6 data types.

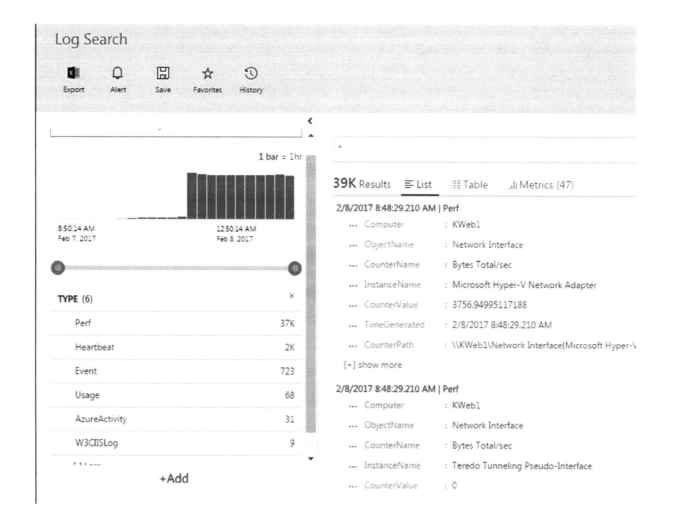

4. In search box input Type=Perf ObjectName=Processor. Now you can see only Performance counter related to processor only.

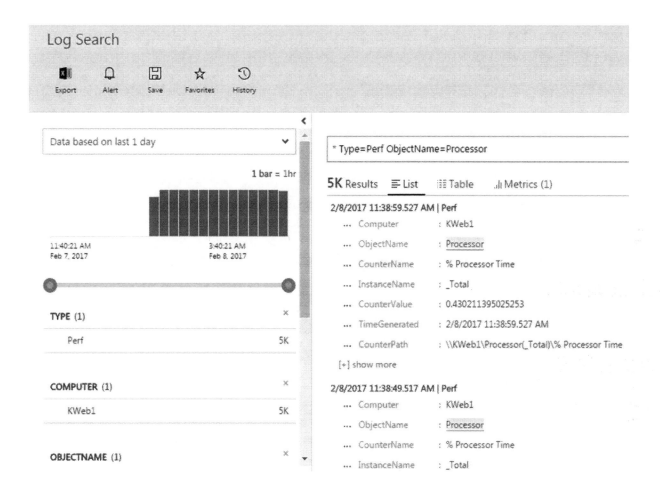

Lab 50: Query IIS Log Data for default website on KWeb1 VM

1. Click Log search tile in OMS Portal> Log search Blade opens>Click All Collected Data>Click W3IISLog in left pane.

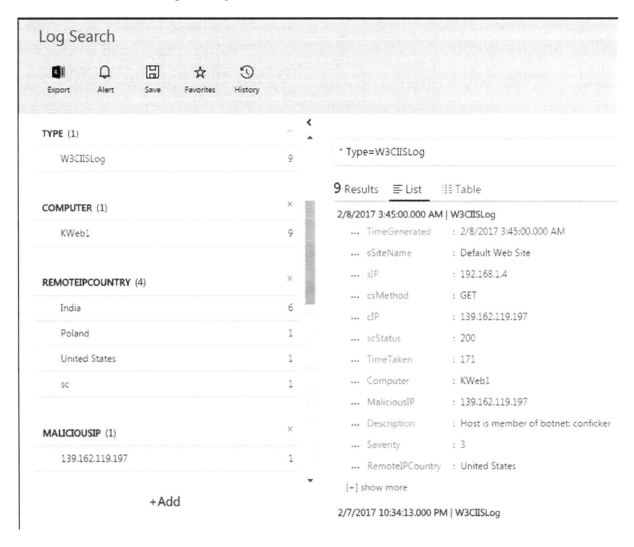

2. The default website on KWeb1 VM has been accessed from 4 countries.
3. There is malicious IP 139.162.119.197 and origin is United Sates.
4. Just Scroll down the left pane and you will see IP addresses of hosts who have accessed this website.

5. Creating Alert rule for IIS Logs. Generate alert when severity is critical>Click alert in W3IISLog pane.

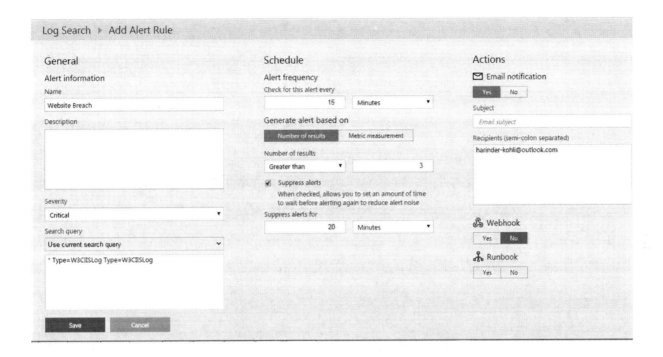

Lab 51: Management Solutions

Management solutions extend the functionality of Operations Management Suite (OMS) by providing packaged management scenarios that customers can add to their environment.Most management solutions require an <u>OMS workspace to</u> contain views.
Management solutions provided by Microsoft can be installed from the Solutions Gallery

1. Log in to the OMS portal@ **https://koms.portal.mms.microsoft.com**
2. Click Solution Gallery Tile. We will install multiple solutions here.

3. Click Insight and Analytics Tile. Click Add.

4. Similarly add Security and Compliance, Protection & Recovery, AD Assessment, Activity Log Analytics, Azure Network Security Group Analytics & Antimalware Assessment.
5. OMS Portal Home Screen after adding Management Solutions.

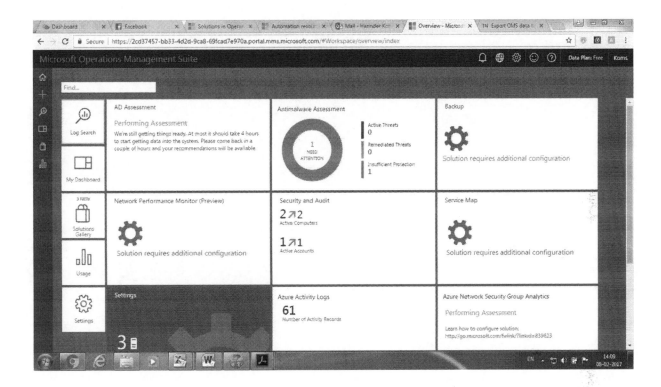

6. I leave it as an exercise for the readers to drill down on each Management solution. After adding Management solutions there are now 10 Data types in log search instead of 6 earlier.

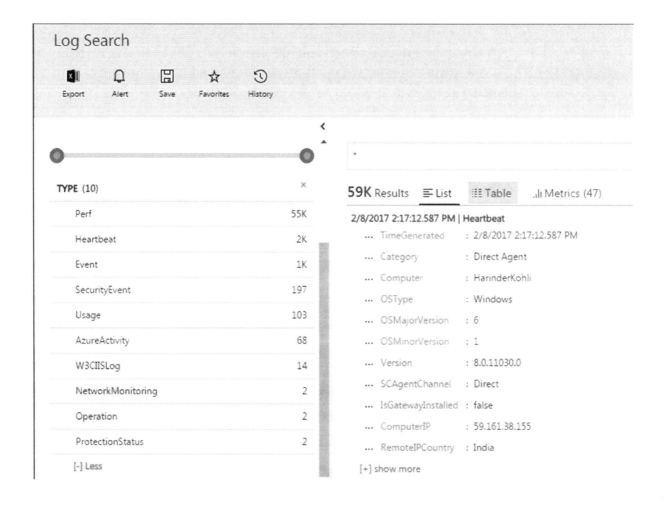

Security and Compliance

Security and Compliance helps you identify, assess, and mitigate security risks to your infrastructure. These features of OMS are implemented through multiple solutions in Log Analytics that analyze log data and configuration from agent systems.

The **Security and Audit solution** collects and analyzes security events on managed systems to identify suspicious activity.

The **Antimalware solution** reports on the status of antimalware protection on managed systems.

The **System Updates solution** performs an analysis of the security updates and other updateson your managed systems so that you easily identify systems requiring patching.

Important Note: In Lab 50 we installed Security and Compliance Solution throughSolution gallery. It consisted of Security and Audit solution & Antimalware solution.

In case it is not installed just go to OMS Portal>Solution Gallery Tile>Click Security and Compliance> click add.

Lab 52: Security And Audit

1. Log in to the OMS portal@ https://koms.portal.mms.microsoft.com
2. Click Security and Audit Tile.

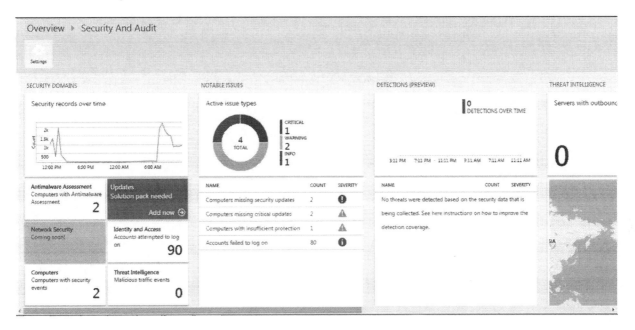

3. Lets click Identity & Access Tile. You can see both successful and failed logon attempts.

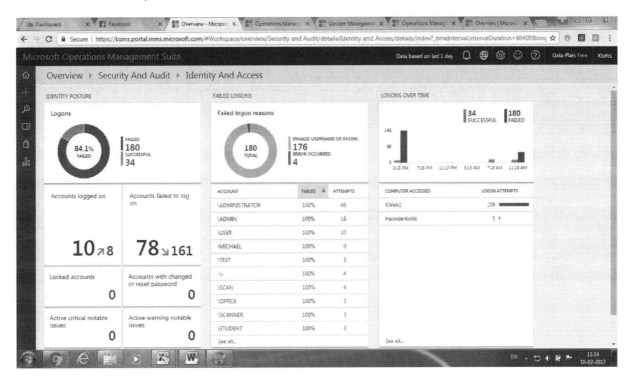

4. As an exercise Readers can go through various options.

Lab 53: Antimalware Assessment

1. Log in to the OMS portal@ https://koms.portal.mms.microsoft.com
2. Click Antimalware Assessment Tile.

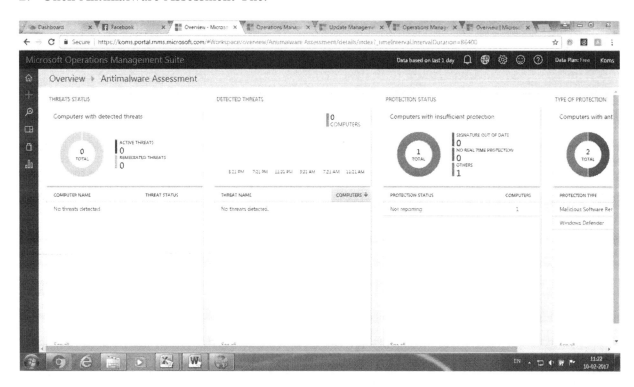

3. Here you can see detected threats, Protection status etc.

Chapter 11 - Web App

Web Apps is a fully managed compute platform that is optimized for hosting websites and web applications.
The Diagram below shows the difference between Azure VMs and Azure Web App.
The boxes with Dark grey color are managed by Azure Cloud.

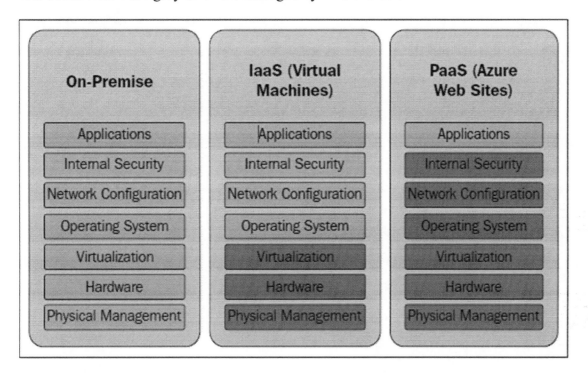

Web App instance can host web applications written in many languages including: ASP.NET, Ruby, Python & Java etc.

Supports continuous integration and deployment with Visual Studio Team Services, GitHub etc.

Can Scale out without configuring any Load Balancers.

Web App have deployment Slot option where you can test your website and if ok you canchange it with production slot without any downtime.

Azure Web Apps come in Five Tiers - Free, Shared, Basic, Standard & Premium.

In this chapter we will add Web App to the topology.

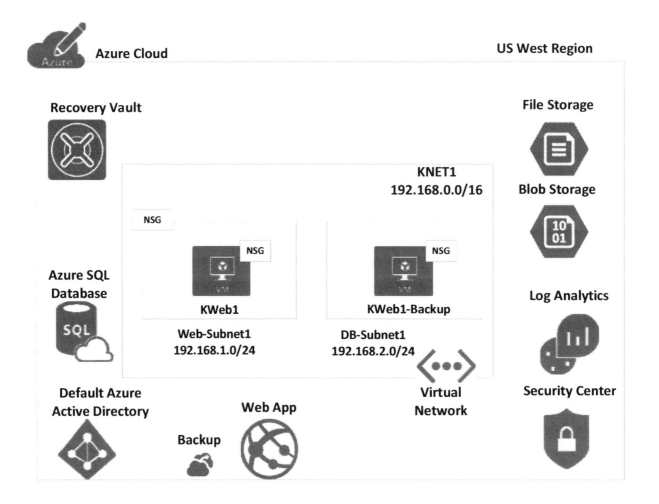

We will create following in Azure Web App Lab:

1. Create Web app and upload custom website.
2. Create staging slot and swapping it with production slot.
3. Configuring Web App options like backup, Authentication etc.

Lab 54: Deploy Web App

1. Click +New>Web+Mobile>Web App.>Specify following in Web App Blade. For App Service Plan select the default>Click create.

2. Go to Kwebapp1 Dashboard.

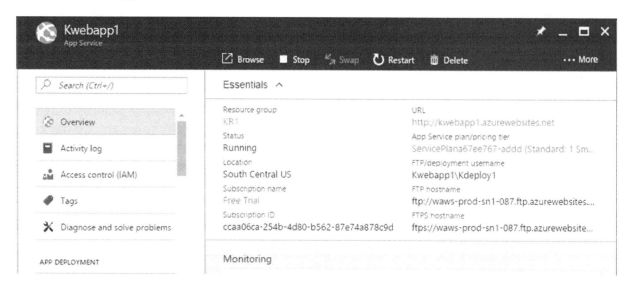

3. Copy URL and http://kwebapp1.azurewebsites.net. Default Website opens.

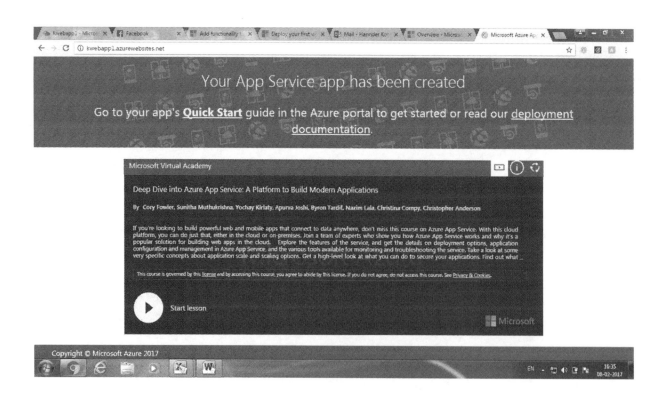

Lab 55: Add Deployment Credentials

FTP can't authenticate using the account you re signed in with, so create a new user name and password to use with FTP.
Use this user name and password to deploy to any apps for all subscriptions associated with your Microsoft Azure account.

1. Go to Kwebapp1 Dashboard> Click Deployment Credential in left pane and specify following and click save.

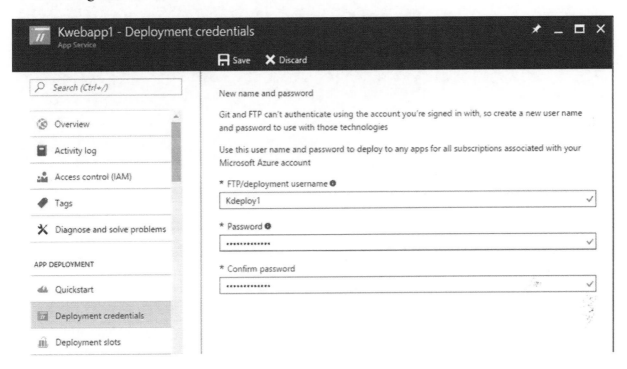

Lab 56: Web App Console

1. Kwebapp1 dashboard>Console.

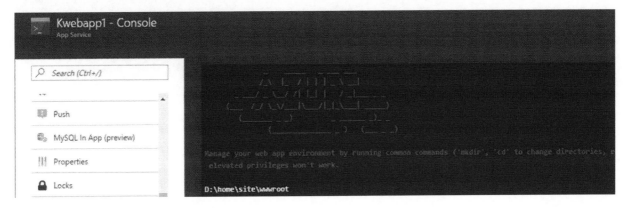

2. Lets create a test directory> mkdir test>cd test (to confirm).

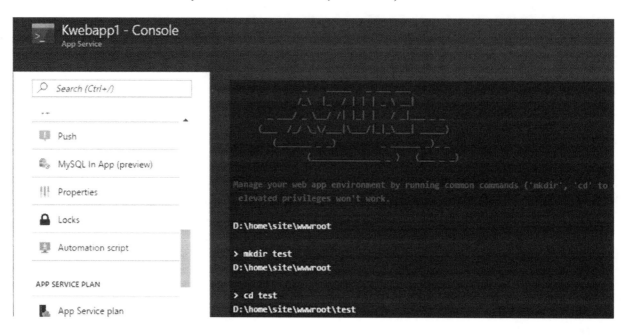

Lab 57: Creating custom website and uploading to Web App

1. In this lab we will upload Index.html file to web App using FileZilla Client for Windows 64bit.
2. Download and Install FileZila Client from **https://filezilla-project.org/download.php**
3. Create a Notepad file and enter following and save the file as index.html on desktop.

```
<!DOCTYPE html>
<html>
<head>
<title>Lab Guide</title>
<meta charset="utf-8">
</head>
<body>
<h1>Hello Azure Cloud. Lab Guide for 70-534: Architecting Microsoft Azure Solutions</h1>
<p> This is Hands on Lab guide on how to use Azure Cloud and prepare for 70-534 exam</p>
</body>
</html>
```

4. Open FileZilla Client>File>Site Manager>New Site> Enter a name. In my case Azure Test. In Host name enter ftp hostname, user as FTP/Deployment username as seen in Kwebapp1 Dashboard. Click connect.

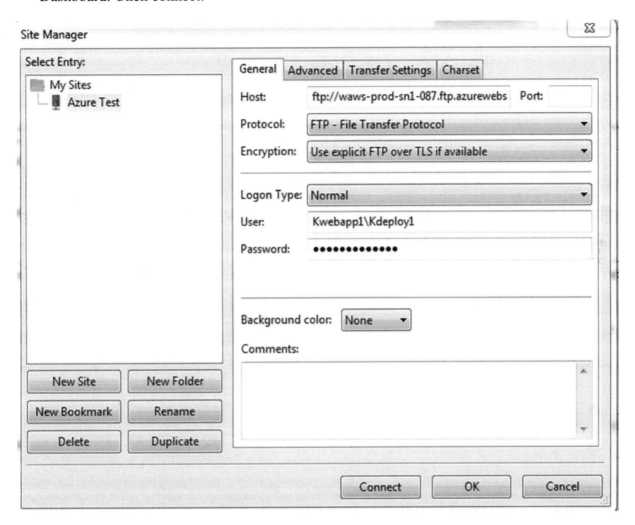

5. Kwebapp1 Dashboard. Note FTP Username and FTP Hostname.

Essentials ︿

Resource group	URL
KR1	http://kwebapp1.azurewebsites.net
Status	App Service plan/pricing tier
Running	ServicePlana67ee767-addd (Standard: 1 Sm...
Location	FTP/deployment username
South Central US	Kwebapp1\Kdeploy1
Subscription name	FTP hostname
Free Trial	ftp://waws-prod-sn1-087.ftp.azurewebsites...
Subscription ID	FTPS hostname
ccaa06ca-254b-4d80-b562-87e74a878c9d	ftps://waws-prod-sn1-087.ftp.azurewebsite...

6. If connected you will see the screen below. There is Remote Site window in top right and /
    folder. Expand the / folder and then expand site folder and you will see wwwroot folder.
    Click on wwwroot folder and you can see test directory which we created in earlier lab and
    default html file hostingstart.html.

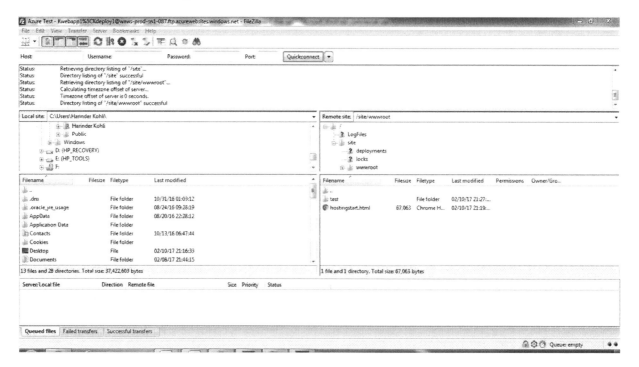

7. We will drag index.html file from our desktop to wwwroot folder. You can now see
    index.html file.

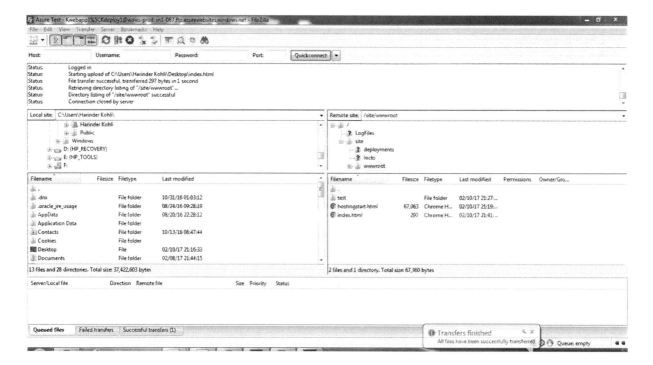

8. Open Browser **https://kwebapp1.azurewebsites.net/.**
9. Make sure to refresh browser with f5.

Hello Azure Cloud. Lab Guide for 70-534: Architecting Microsoft Azure Solutions

This is Hands on Lab guide on how to use Azure Cloud and prepare for 70-534 exam.

10. Instead of Default web site hostingstart.html **we now have index.html**.

Lab 58: Set up staging environments by creating Deployment Slot

When you deploy your web app, you can deploy it to a separate deployment slot instead of the default production slot. You can validate app changes in a staging deployment slot before swapping it with the production slot.

1. **Create Deployment Slot**>Kwebapp1 dashboard>Deployment Slots>Click +Add>Specify Following>Click Ok.

2. Kwebapp1 dashboard>Deployment Slots> click staging deployment slot to open slot's resource blade>Staging Web App Dashboard opens.

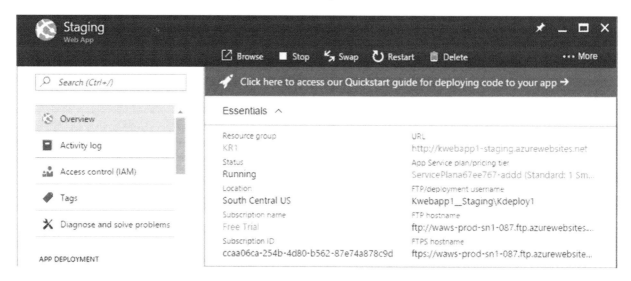

3. Copy staging web app URL and http://kwebapp1-staging.azurewebsites.net. Default web site opens.

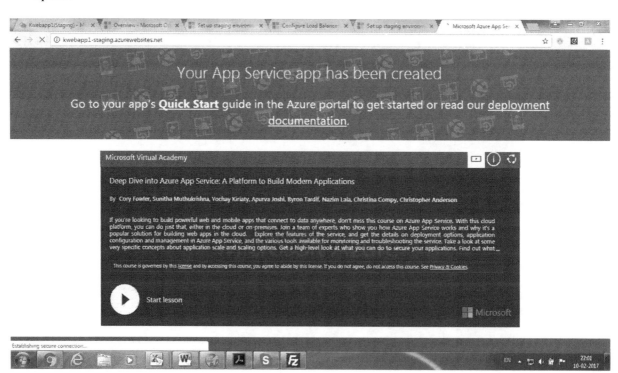

4. **Swap Staging deployment slots with Production slot.** Go to Staging Web app dashboard>Click swap>swap blade opens>specify following>ok.

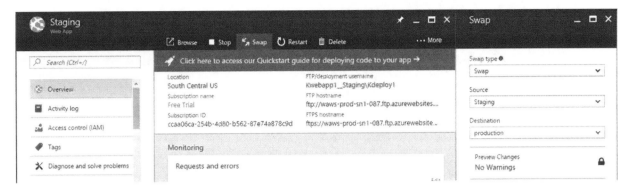

5. Copy the URL of Kwebapp1 and **http://kwebapp1.azurewebsites.net/**. Note: It is no longer showing the custom website we created in earlier lab. It is showing the default website of staging web app.

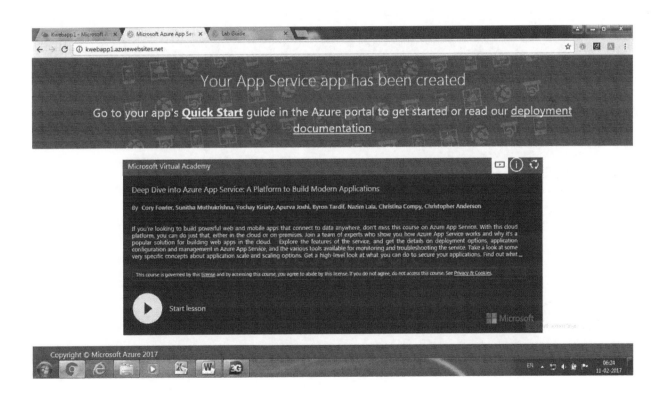

6. Copy the URL of staging web App and **http://kwebapp1-staging.azurewebsites.net/**

Hello Azure Cloud. Lab Guide for 70-534: Architecting Microsoft Azure Solutions

This is Hands on Lab guide on how to use Azure Cloud and prepare for 70-534 exam

7. It is no longer showing default website.**This means staging Web App is in production slot.**

8. FTP using Kwebapp1 ftp username. Lets see whether it connects to Kwebapp1 or Staging.
   FTP Username of staging Webapp: Kwebapp1__Staging\Kdeploy1
   FTP Username of KWebapp1 Webapp: Kwebapp1\Kdeploy1

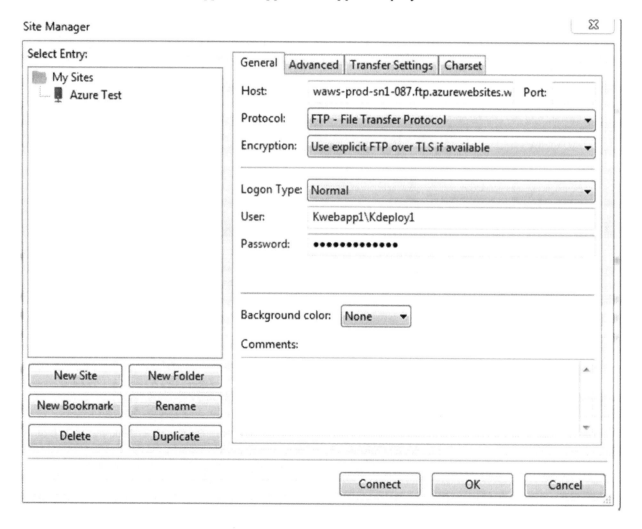

9. You can see it is no longer showing index.html & Test folder in wwwroot folder. This means **Staging Web App is in production slot.**

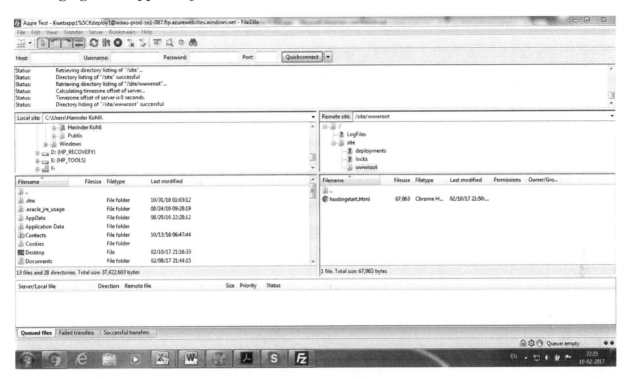

10. As an exercise to readers reverse back staging webapp in production slot back to Staging deployment slot.

Lab 59: Creating Backup

1. Kwebapp1 dashboard>Backups

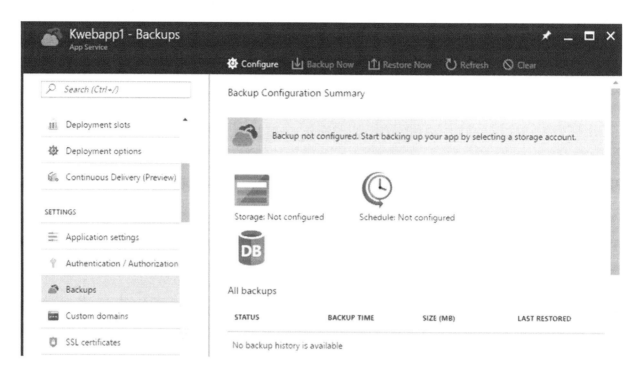

2. Click Storage Not Configured. Select Kstorgps1. Select Kstorgps1 again and click select.

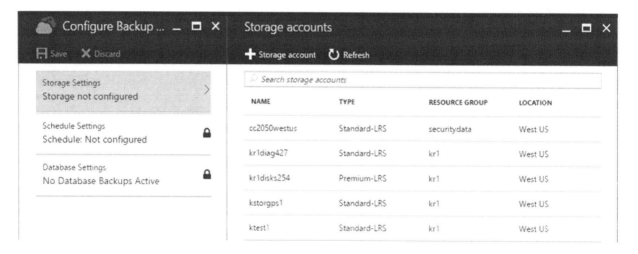

3. Click Schedule settings. Select on. Click Ok.

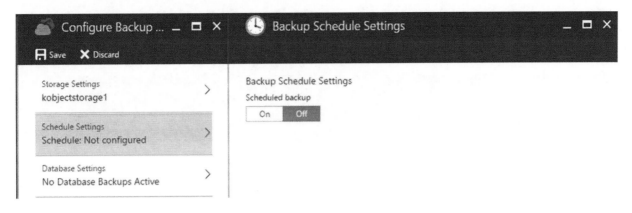

4. Click save. Now you can see Backup is configured.

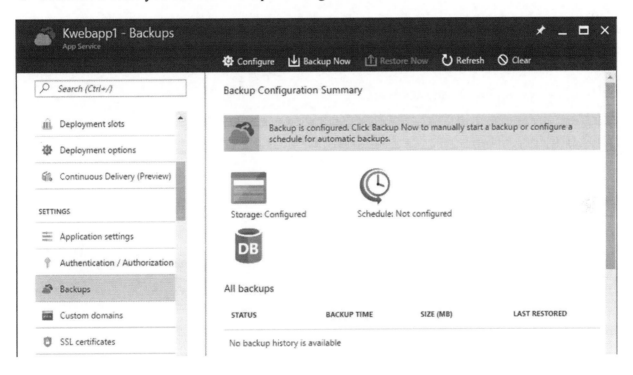

5. You can click Backup Now to start backup.

Lab 60: Add Authentication/Authorization using AAD

1. Go to KWebapp1 dashboard and click Authentication/Authorization in left pane and specify following.

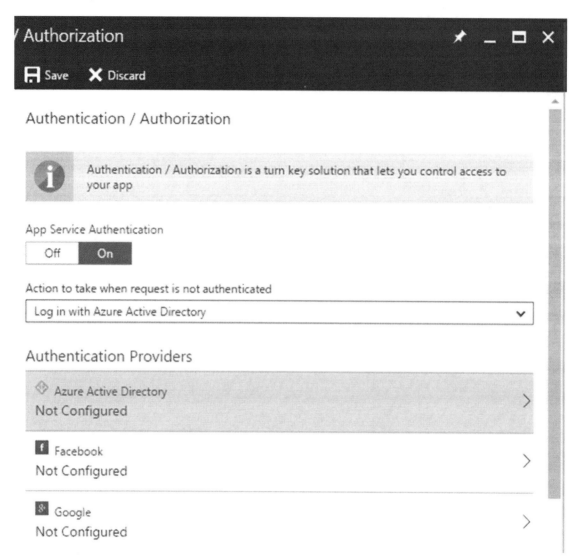

2. Under Authorization Providers click Azure Active Directory and specify following.

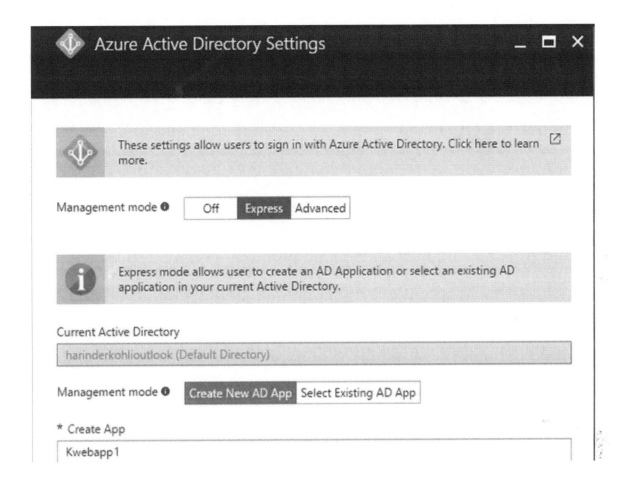

3. Click Ok and then save.

4. Open Kwebapp1 URL http://kwebapp1.azurewebsites.net in another web browser. If you are using chrome for admin then open with IE.

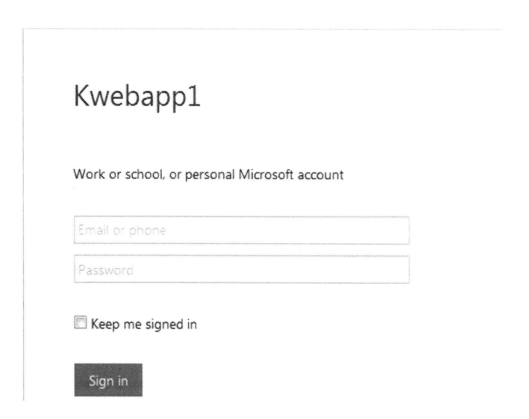

Kwebapp1

Work or school, or personal Microsoft account

Email or phone

Password

☐ Keep me signed in

Sign in

5. Website is asking for Authentication.

Lab 61: Performance Test

This will do performance test on Kwebapp1 website with a load of 250 users and will determine website average response time under full load. It will also test the CPU and Memory under full load. Based on these 2 information you can select the right Web App tier for your Webapp and/or choose Autoscaling with right minimum instances.

Note it will take close to 10-15 minutes to acquire resources and start the test. You can change the number of users and duration of test as per your requirement.

1. Kwebapp1 Dashboard>click Performance Test in left pane>Click +New>New Performance Test Blade opens>specify following>click Run Test.

2. **Monitor test**. Kwebapp1 Dashboard>click Performance Test in left pane>Click the test created which is PerfTest01 in this case>PerfTest01 blade opens.

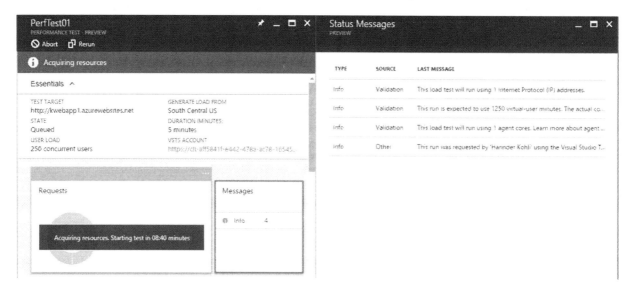

3. It is showing that it is acquiring resources.
4. Scroll down and you will see performance graph under full load and CPU & Memory graph.
5. Performance Graphs and CPU & Memory Graph after test is completed.

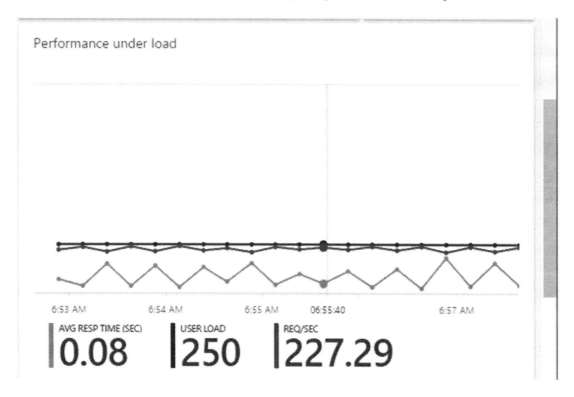

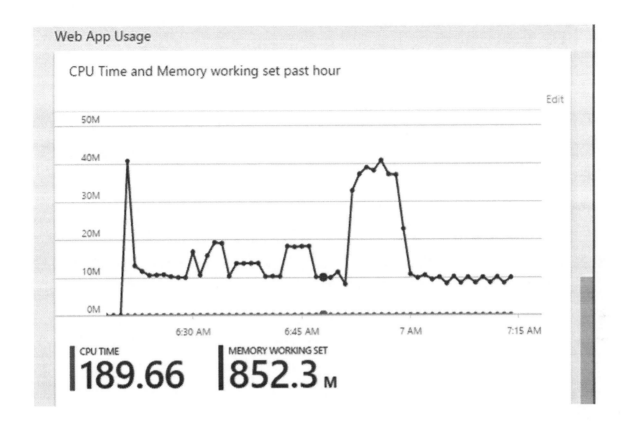

Additional labs

There is so much to do in Web Apps. Readers should do some more labs like adding custom domain name, Autoscaling, Alert Rule, Application insights, Cloud deployment option using onedrive, dropbox etc, continuous deployment.

Chapter 12 - Load Balancing

Microsoft Azure offers three types of load Balancers: Azure Load Balancer, Application Gateway & Traffic Manager.

Azure Load Balancer is a Layer 4 (TCP, UDP) load balancer that distributes incoming traffic among healthy instances of services defined in a load-balanced set.

Application Gateway works at the application layer. It acts as a reverse-proxy service, terminating the client connection and forwarding requests to back-end endpoints.

Traffic Manager works at the DNS level. It uses DNS responses to direct end-user traffic to globally distributed endpoints. Clients then connect to those endpoints directly.

Azure Load Balancer can probe the health of the various server instances using probes. When a probe fails to respond, the load balancer stops sending new connections to the unhealthy instances.

All outbound traffic to the Internet that originates from your service undergoes source NAT (SNAT) by using the same VIP address as the incoming traffic.

In Hash-based distribution mode, Packets in the same session will be directed to the same datacenter IP (DIP) instance behind the load balanced endpoint. When the client starts a new session from the same source IP, the source port changes and causes the traffic to go to a different DIP endpoint.

In Source IP affinity distribution mode, connections initiated from the same client computer goes to the same datacenter IP (DIP) endpoint.

In this chapter we will add Azure Load Balancer to the Topology.

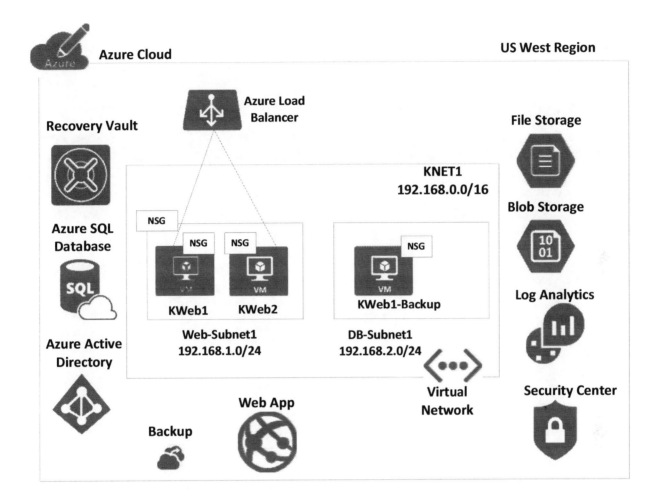

We will create following in Azure Load Balancer Lab:

1. Create VM KWeb2 and Load Balancer
2. Load balance default website traffic on KWeb1 and KWeb2 using Load Balancer.

Lab 62: Create Windows Server VM KWeb2 and enable IIS

1. We will use this VM along with Kweb1 VM created earlier to test Load Balancing.
2. Log on to **http://portal.azure.com**
3. Click +New>Compute>Windows Server 2016 Datacenter>Select Resource Manager and click create>create Virtual Machine Blade opens>specify following.

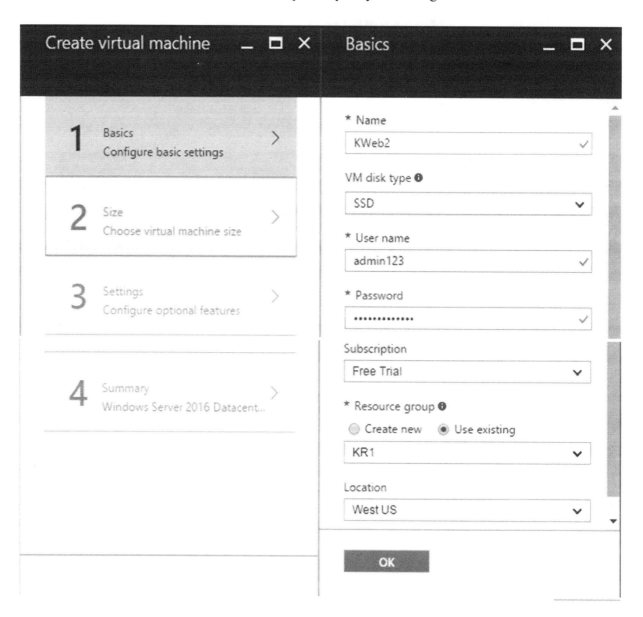

4. In create virtual machine blade size settings click View All and Select DS1_V2.

5. In create virtual machine blade settings select default values for storage account, Public IP Address, Network Security group, Monitoring & Guest OS. For Availability Set select KAS1.

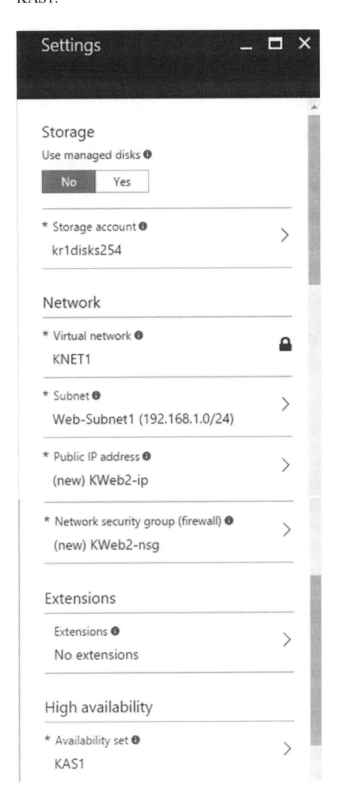

Note: Managed Disk Option. This was not there when we created KWeb1 VM.

6. Click Ok in summary settings. It will take few minutes for deployment to complete.
7. KWeb2 VM dashboard>click connect and download RDP with IP address of KWeb2 VM.
8. Connect to KWeb2 VM using RDP.
9. Open server Manager> Click add roles and features
10. In the Add Roles and Features Wizard, on the Installation Type page, choose Role-based or feature-based installation, and then click Next.
11. Select KWeb2 VM from the server pool and click Next.
12. On the Server Roles page, select Web Server (IIS).
13. In the pop-up about adding features needed for IIS, make sure that Include management tools is selected and then click Add Features. When the pop-up closes, click Next in the wizard.
14. next, next, next, next.
15. Install.
16. It will take around 1 minute to install the IIS. After Installation is complete click close.

Lab 63: Adding http inbound rule in the KWeb2 VM NSG

1. **https://portal.azure.com**
2. Click All Resources>Select and click Network Security group KWeb2-nsg> Click Inbound security Rules>Click +Add>Specify following and click ok.

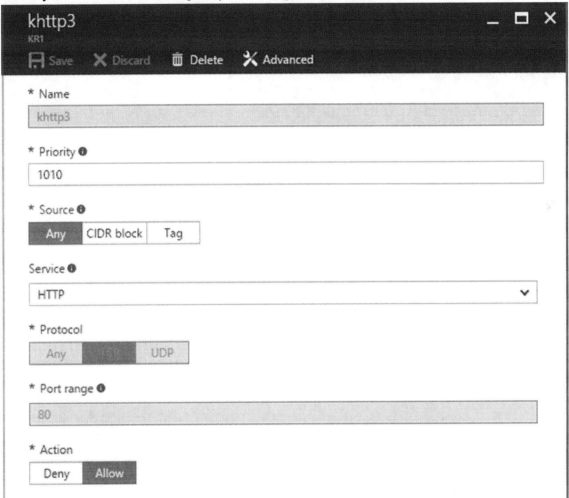

3. Check the default website in KWeb2 VM>Copy the KWeb2 IP which is 13.64.237.7> http:// 13.64.237.7>Default website works.

Lab 64: Creating Internet Facing Load Balancer

1. Log on to **http://portal.azure.com**
2. Click +New>Networking>Load Balancer>Create Load Balancer Blade opens. Specify following and click create. For Public IP address create KIP1.

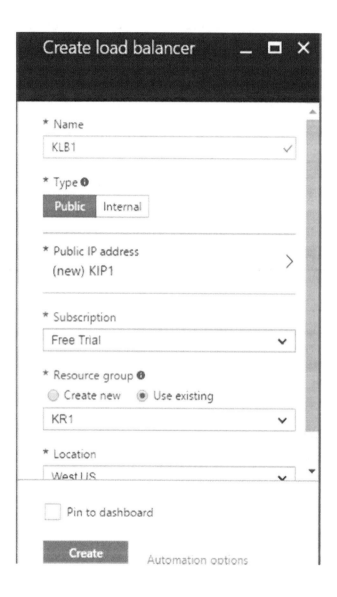

Lab 65: Create a back-end address pool

1. **This will add end points which are to be load balanced.**
2. Load Balancer KLB1 Dashboard>Click Backend Pools in left Pane.

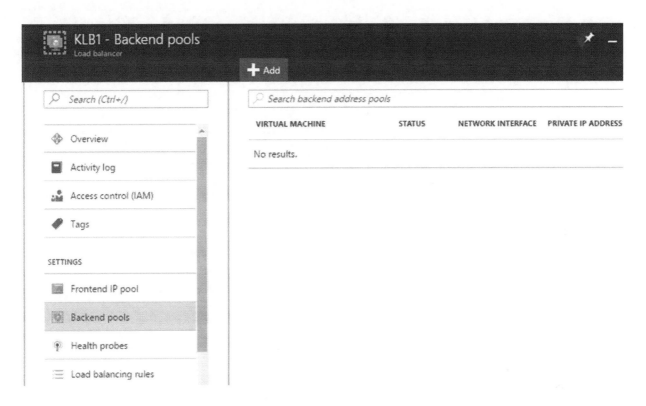

3. Click +Add>Add Backend pool blade opens>Specify following.

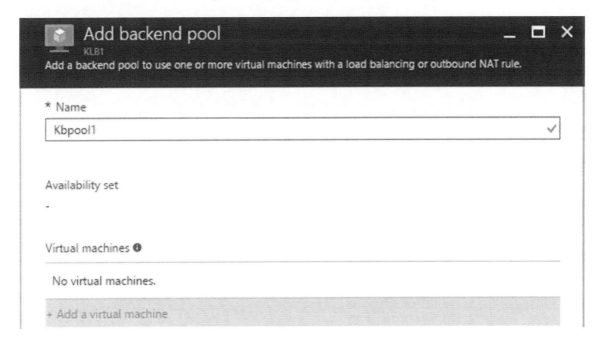

4. click +Add a Virtual Machine >Choose Virtual Machine blade opens>specify following> Click select>click ok. Remember to select availability set.

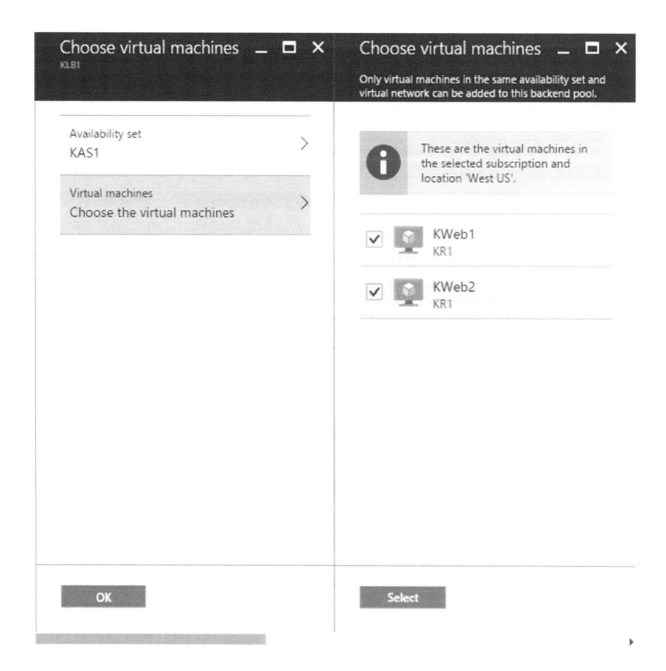

Lab 66: Create a Health probe

1. **Health Probes are used to check the health status of the endpoints.** If endpoint does not responds to probes, Load balancer will stop sending traffic to that endpoint.
2. Load Balancer KLB1 Dashboard>Click Health Probes in left Pane>Click +Add>Add health Probe blade opens>specify following and click ok.

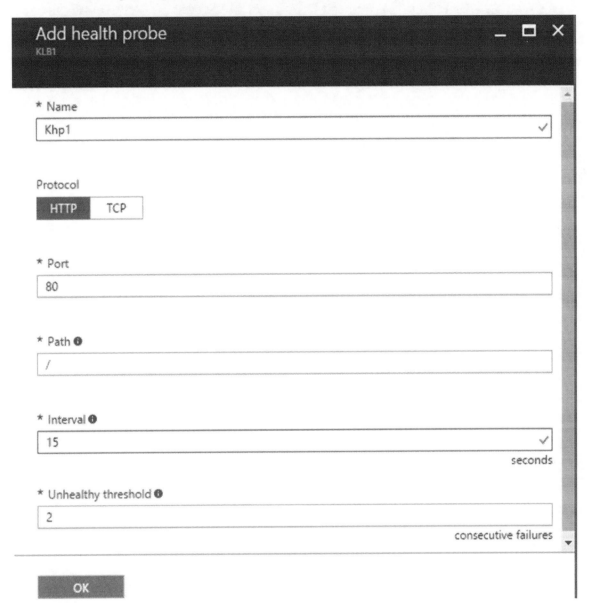

Lab 67: Create a Load Balancing Rule

1. Load Balancer KLB1 Dashboard>Click Load Balancing Rules in left Pane>Click +Add>Add Load Balancing Rule blade opens>specify following and click ok.

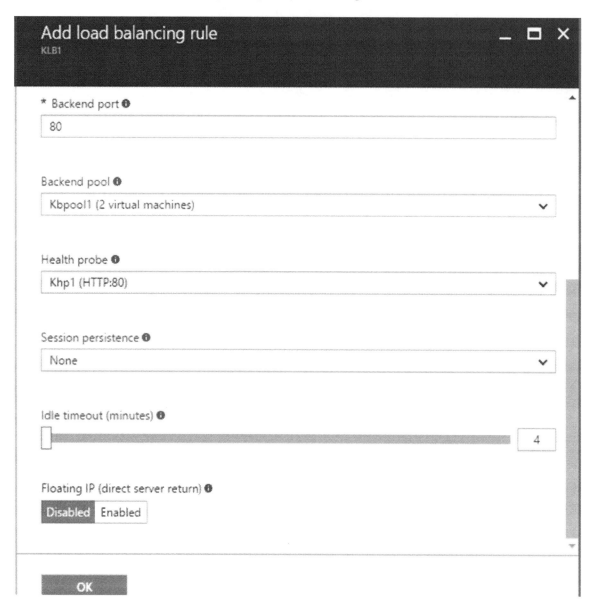

Lab 68: Create a Inbound NAT Rule

1. Load Balancer KLB1 Dashboard>Click Inbound NAT Rules in left Pane>Click +Add>Add inbound NAT Rule blade opens>specify following and click ok.

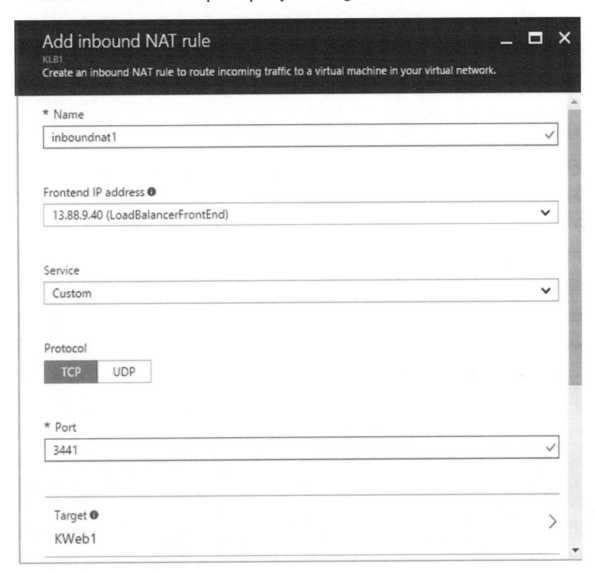

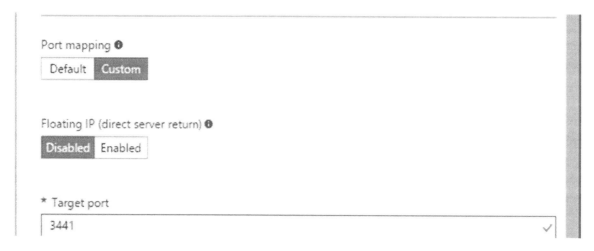

Port mapping ⓘ

Default | **Custom**

Floating IP (direct server return) ⓘ

Disabled | Enabled

* Target port

3441 ✓

2. Repeat above step to create inboundnat2 rule and select target as KWeb2 VM and port 3442.

Lab 69: Access the default website on KWeb1 and KWeb2 using Load Balancer IP

1. Load Balancer KLB1 Dashboard>copy Load Balancer IP which is 13.88.9.40.
2. Open Browser and **http://13.88.9.40/**

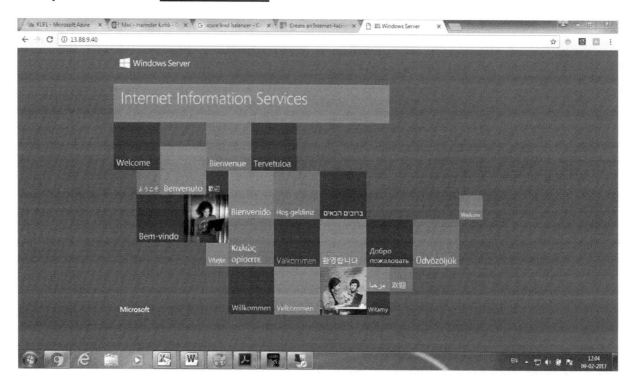

3. Access the website couple of times through different browsers.

Lab 70: Add KWeb2 to Log Analytics to check for IIS Logs

Note: We will add KWeb2 VM to log Analytics and then in log Search see whether IIS logs are being generated or not when website is accessed through Load Balancer. In this lab we will install Log Analytics VM extension on KWeb2.

1. Go to log Analytics Dashboard Koms>Click Virtual Machines. It shows KWeb2 not connected.

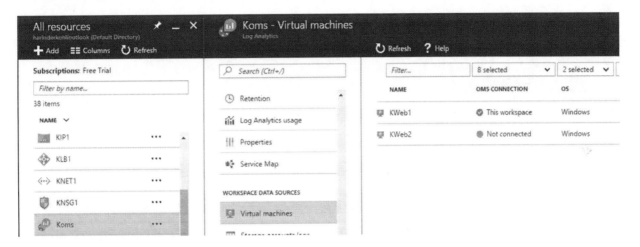

2. Click KWeb2 Virtual Machine> KWeb2 VM Blade opens> Click Connect.

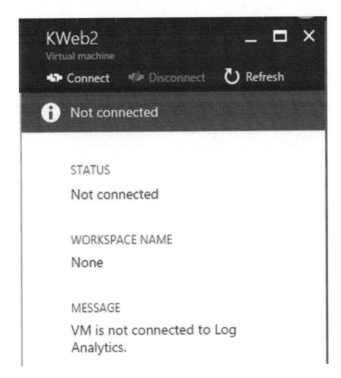

3. Log on to OMS portal by going to **https://koms.portal.mms.microsoft.com**

4. Click Log search in OMS Portal> Log search Blade opens> Click All Collected Data>Click W3IISLog in left pane. You can see IIS Logs are being generated for KWeb2.

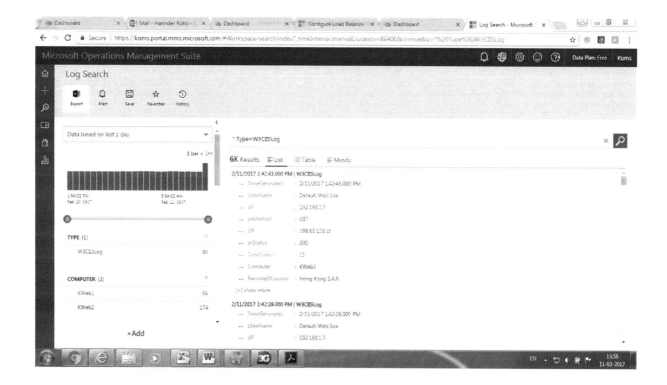

Chapter 13 - Global Load Balancing with Traffic Manager

Traffic Manager works at the DNS level. It uses DNS responses to direct end-user traffic to globally distributed endpoints. Clients then connect to those endpoints directly.

Endpoints supported by Traffic Manager include Azure VMs, Web Apps, Cloud Services and Non Azure Endpoints.Traffic Manager also supports Azure Load Balancers as Endpoints.

Traffic Manager uses the Domain Name System (DNS) to direct client requests to the most appropriate endpoint based on a **traffic-routing method** and the health of the endpoints.

Three Traffic routing methods are available in Traffic Manager.

Priority: when you want to use a primary service endpoint for all traffic, and provide backups in case the primary or the backup endpoints are unavailable.
Weighted: when you want to distribute traffic across a set of endpoints, either evenly or according to weights, which you define.
Performance: when you have endpoints in different geographic locations and you want end users to use the "closest" endpoint in terms of the lowest network latency.

Note: Traffic Manager is usually combined with other Azure Load Balancing solutions.

Case Study: Combining Load Balancing Services

You can Combine Traffic Manager with Azure Application Gateway and Azure Load Balancer. For Example you want EMEA users to go to Website in Europe and APAC & US users to go to website in US. You want layer 7 load balancing and session affinity. Traffic Manager Does not support session Affinity. Traffic Manager will direct users to respective Application Gateway based on performance routing method and Application Gateway will then load balance Website in each region and provide session affinity.

In this chapter we will add Azure Traffic Manager to the Topology.

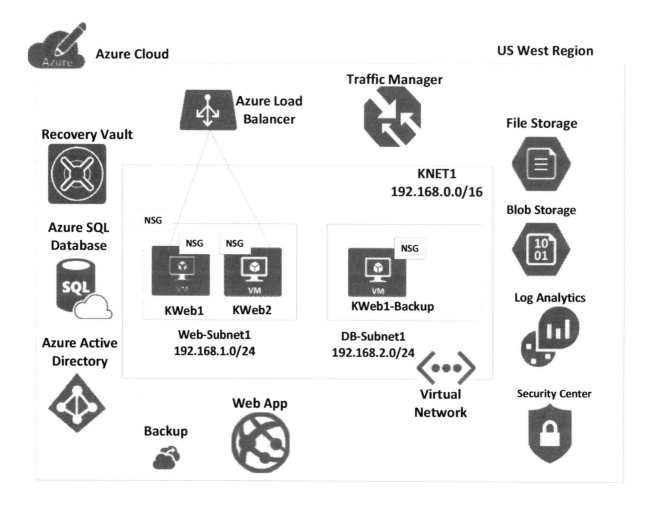

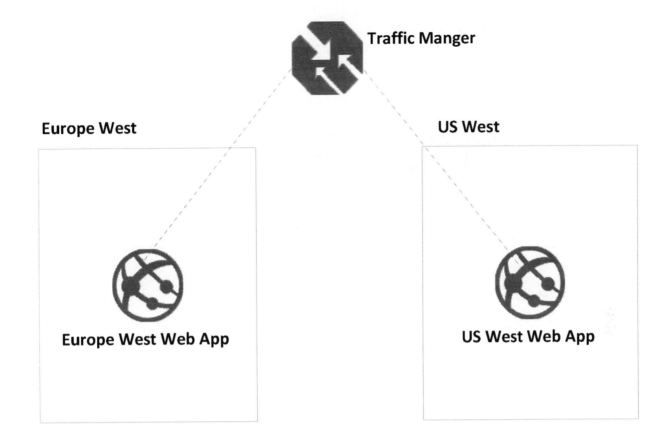

Traffic Manger

Europe West

US West

Europe West Web App

US West Web App

We will create following in Azure Traffic Manager Lab.

1. Create Web App in Europe West and US West
2. Create Traffic Manager Profile
3. Load balance Europe and US Web App using Traffic Manager

Lab 71: Deploy Web App in Europe West

1. Click +New>Web+Mobile>Web App.>Specify following in Web App Blade. For App Service Plan create new Plan **stds1eu** in Europe West Location and click Ok> click create.

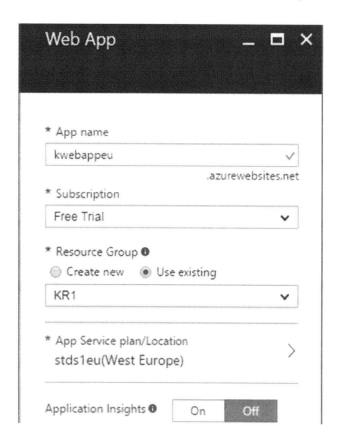

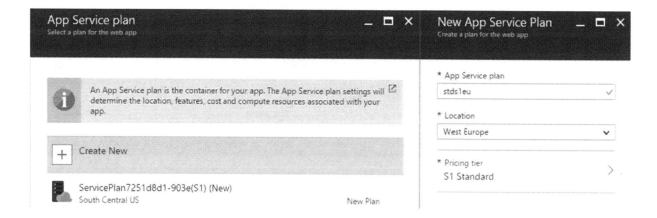

2. Upload Index.html file to web App kwebappeu using FileZilla Client. I have already shown the process of uploading file in Lab 57.

Lab 72: Deploy Web App in US West

1. Click +New>Web+Mobile>Web App.>Specify following in Web App Blade. For App Service Plan create new Plan stds1uswest in US WEST location and click Ok> click create.

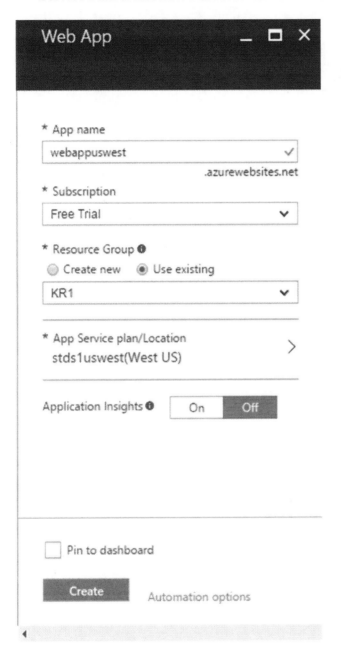

Lab 73: Create Traffic Manager Profile

1. Azure Portal>Click + New > In the search box type traffic manager and Press enter.
2. Insearch result choose traffic manager profile>Click create>create TM profile blde opens>specify following and click create.

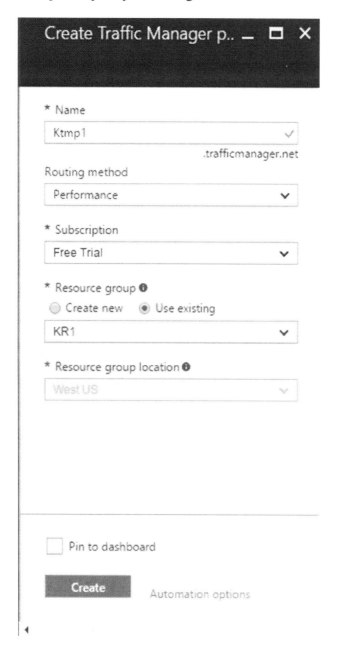

3. I selected Routing Method as Performance. I suggest readers go with weighted because everybody would not have Tor Browser installed.

Lab 74: Add Endpoints in Traffic Manager Profile

1. **Add Endpoint Europe West Web App kwebappeu.** Traffic Manager Ktmp1 dashboard> click endpoints>+Add>Add endpoint blade opens>specify following and click create.

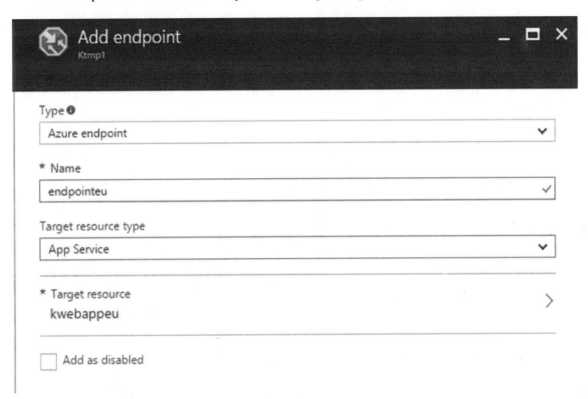

2. **Add Endpoint US West Web App webappuswest.** Traffic Manager Ktmp1 dashboard> click endpoints>+Add>Add endpoint blade opens>specify following and click create.

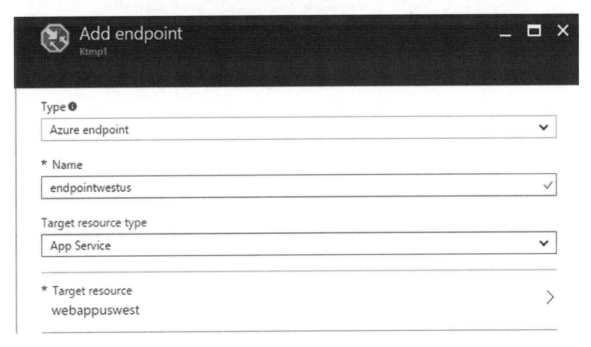

Lab 75: Test The Load Balancing

Note 1: Here I will use 2 Browsers. One Chrome and second TOR Browser which will connect through a European node.
Note 2: US West Web App has default website
Note 3: Europe West has index.html website.

1. Open Chrome Browser and **http://ktmp1.trafficmanager.net/**
2. It opens Web App default website. This is our US West location as Europe West has index.html website.

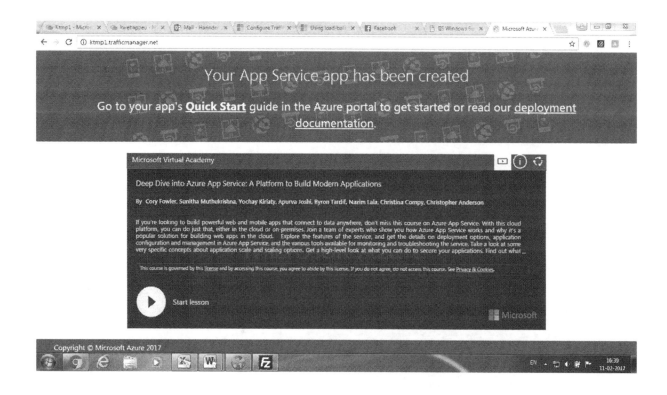

3. Open TOR Browser and connect through a European node.
   http://ktmp1.trafficmanager.net/. It opens index.html file which is our Europe West Web
   App.

Hello Azure Cloud. Lab Guide for 70-534: Architecting Microsoft Azure Solutions

This is Hands on Lab guide on how to use Azure Cloud and prepare for 70-534 exam.